The Gospel of Pandemonium

Edward Pandemonium

© Copyright 2019 by Horngate Media

All rights reserved. No part of this book may be reproduced, transmitted, or utilized, in any form or by any means, electronic or mechanical, including photocopying, recording, or by any information storage and retrieval system, without written permission from the author or publisher, except for brief quotations in critical articles, books, and reviews.

First edition published by
Horngate Media
New Port Richey, FL 34653
USA

ISBN: 978-0-9909700-0-2

Book Layout & Pre-Press:
Philip H. Farber
http://www.hawkridgeproductions.com

Cover Design:
Hagen von Tulien
https://www.behance.net/Hagen_von_Tulien

"So shall my word be that goeth forth out of my mouth: it shall not return unto me void, but it shall accomplish that which I please, and it shall prosper in the thing whereto I sent it." - Isaiah 55:11

To Anastasia, for giving me the Mandala.

CONTENTS

1. Into the Aeons... 1
2. The Daemonic Invasion............................ 7
3. Nuit.. 11
4. Hadit... 49
5. Ra-Hoor-Khuit.. 73
6. Summa... 103
7. The Princess... 107
8. The Discovery and Recovery of Xaryomen.. 113
9. The Xaryomen Mandala........................... 121
10. The Mass of Xaryomen............................ 125
11. The Foundations of Nobility.................... 131

1

Into the Aeons

In his essay "The Unknown Known", Anton LaVey presents a scheme of historical cycles based upon multiples of the number 9. He calls the most basic of these a Working, a period of eighteen years. The midway point of this period represents a zenith of intensity for the component forces of that Working, which are explicated and integrated over the second half of the period.

When I realized that the completion of my own first Working with the formula of Pandemonium was approaching, I planned several activities that would help me to both celebrate what was past and open the way for the next cycle. One of these activities, particular to being a Setian, was to explore the relationship between Set and Horus in greater depth. This included a series of operations at their appropriate anniversary dates throughout the year to interact with the sources or roots of the Aeon of Horus, Age of Satan and Aeon of Set. With Thelema having been an important part of my distant past, this also gave a me a fun opportunity to revisit part of my youth with older eyes.

During the Thelemic phase, part of my process was to ritually engage with the appropriate entity from *Liber AL vel Legis*, then read the corresponding chapter and jot down my thoughts. Later, I read the various commentaries by Aleister Crowley, as well as those by

THE GOSPEL OF PANDEMONIUM

Michael Aquino, Don Webb and Kenneth Grant. As I found myself also having my own thoughts about those texts, I decided to try my hand at my own full commentary. My thought was to see what new perspectives and powers, if any, might be drawn from the Book of the Law after all these years and so much ink under the bridge. This was purely an exercise for myself, and you will see that the result is very much my own - almost solipsistically so in parts - but I did feel that parts of it might be of use to others. As I shared various drafts and selections with intimates and colleagues, I was increasingly persuaded that it might be magically desirable to release it to the wider world and encouraged to do so.

What I have done is to comment upon the Book, itself, its previous commentaries, the historical evolution of ideas through the manifestations of the Age of Satan and Aeon of Set, and finally ground it all in the context of the Black Earth of Pandemonium.

Much of the newly revealed message and import can be gained from an initial, simple reading. However, to fully understand all of my references in the commentary, you are going to need some additional resources. Crowley's own commentaries can be found online, and those by Aquino and Webb have been published in the book *Overthrowing the Old Gods*. Grant's is in his book *Hecate's Fountain*.

For the basic Setian understanding of the relationship between the Aeons of Horus and Set (with the Age of Satan as a period of overlap), the *Book of Coming Forth by Night* has been released to the world in Michael Aquino's *Temple of Set* history. References to the Red Magus, which become increasingly important as my commentary progresses, come from the *Diabolicon*. That text is now available in Aquino's *The Satanic Bible: 50th Anniversary ReVision* (and, of course, Anton Lavey's basic philosophy of Satanism is presented in the original *Satanic Bible*).

Finally, the fundamental Pandemonium text is my book *The Black Ship* (unintentionally produced just when it should have been, nine years earlier), but I am also including the text of an old, printed informational flyer "The Daemonic Invasion" as a brief overview. This and all of these further studies provide more detail to my commentary and place my comments into fuller context.

The message of the Book of the Law has been progressively whitewashed and watered down for more than a century; somewhat by Crowley, himself, and certainly at an ever-quickening pace since his death. This has unfortunately diminished its effectiveness in its purpose of preparing the world for what was and is to come. Now, though, not only is its initial potency restored but even further power is drawn forth from it. One hopes that there is still time to apply it before we are all swept up in the radical world changes of the coming decades.

In this same time period, I have also been working with a personal system derived from Proto-Indo-European mythology and religion. Previously written essays on that very-early-'pagan' influenced work that were circulated privately the year before are now also included here as a complement to the more historically recent material that makes up the first section. This second section is shorter and more straightforward but taps into deep, archetypal forces that should not be seen as more simplistic.

It is not a pure reconstruction and it is not meant to be. Its primary sources are Michael Bertiaux's 'Lucky Hoodoo' system for functionality and Ceisiwr Serith's book *Deep Ancestors* for content. Drawing from Bertiaux may at first seem incongruous to PIE lore but it was that work that drew me further into the PIE realm through Ancestry and the Dead, it was during the period of that work that the Xaryomen Mandala was revealed through the dream of another party, and Bertiaux's mandalic altar and easy methods of interacting with the Spirits were perfect for my needs.

Once I adjusted the layout for color and made the PIE associations, a whole system clicked into place. As explained above, I can only take about a quarter of the credit for the Mass of Xaryomen ritual, itself, and merely as a collagist. Even so, for me, it was one of those fantastic moments in Magic where something new - or very old - seems to come into vital existence of its own accord.

The Xaryomen Mandala described here is not the Pandemonium Mandala referred to in *The Black Ship*. However, the Xaryomen Mandala is not *not* an aspect of that Mandala, either. The Pandemonium Mandala describes the emanation of the Daemons from the Black Sun and their relationship to each other. It relates mostly to the Psychic and Social dimensions of the Pandemonium continuum. I recommend that everyone create their own images of it. The Xaryomen Mandala relates more to the Social and Environmental dimensions, using a primal mythology to define and describe what we might call the House of the

Daemons. It is also just one possible example of an illustrative and operational mandala for that purpose. Both are expressions of the Ur-Mandala, which is the archetypal pattern of wholeness, harmony and well-being.

Following *The Black Ship*, all of my books have been experiments in fleshing out some aspect of Pandemonium that could then be folded back into the broad strokes outlined in the original book. This one comes more directly out of my own story but also engages with forces of broad Aeonic interest and will also be folded back into that original vision. These are some of the choicest magical fruits of Pandemonium's first Working period and are also magical seeds for its next cycle.

2

The Daemonic Invasion

Do you feel like a stranger in a strange land? Do you feel drawn to both the mysteries of the past and the possibilities of the future - but yet stuck in the middle? Have you often felt like you have a special purpose that you need to discover or that you are meant for something very different from the people and places around you?

You may be feeling the PANDEMONIUM IMPERATIVE.

WHAT IS PANDEMONIUM?

Pandemonium is an emerging concept in Left-Hand Path thought and practice that simultaneously refers to a primal and hidden realm of existence, a powerful means for upgrading your personal experience of life and an exciting potential for dramatic cultural change on a global scale - and beyond. The word is Latinized Greek for "All-Daemon-Place" or "Abode of all Daemons" and thus represents the integration of three parts into a whole - a DAEMON, the society of ALL the Daemons and their PLACE or abode. Pandemonium can be seen to define a continuum comprising Individual, social and environmental-material dimensions.

WHO ARE THE DAEMONS?

The key to Pandemonium is what we call Daemonic Integration. You may have heard about "Knowledge and Conversation of the Holy Guardian Angel" but Daemonic Integration is a more precise and practical term with more precise and practical methods. There is a usually hidden but essential and superconscious dimension of being that we call the Daemon. Daemonic Integration is the process of making this dimension of being consciously known and integrating it into daily life, transforming the human persona or character while expanding and intensifying experience. Through Daemonic Integration, we become more whole and concentrated versions of ourselves.

The unique existence of each Individual realized through Daemonic Integration calls for the discovery and EXPRESSION of personal power and a sense of Life Purpose that most fully enhance and fulfill the potential of that existence. In actualizing and fulfilling its potential and sense of purpose, each Individual has a unique process of growth, development or BECOMING to pursue. This is the Individual dimension of Pandemonium.

This can not help but affect our relationships. Old relationships and social ties are likely to become outmoded and unfulfilling, while the strong need to align with others more resonant with our new state becomes imperative. As we become more consciously aware of our Deep Desires and needs and more boldly express and pursue them (what we call Black Heart), we will come into contact with those other Individuals with whom we may more profitably relate. Moreover, from our new relationships, we form larger networks and even new sovereign institutions to enhance and maintain our new development, affinities and relationships. This is the social dimension of Pandemonium.

WHERE IS PANDEMONIUM?

New and concentrated states of being and new and intensified relationships are sure to also seek reflection in material culture. We will apply the fullness of our creativity to the spaces, technology and other material wealth that we control to create and maintain enclaves that support our networks and institutions as well as satisfying our needs for aesthetic nourishment and wonder. Start with your own home and work outwards.

Spiritually, Pandemonium provides a Left-Hand Path counterpoint to the various Right-Hand Path ideas of "The Kingdom" or "World to Come" that you have probably heard before. However, rather than waiting and watching for prophetic scripts to be acted out by external powers, Pandemonium is about the Self in the Here and Now. Creatively, Pandemonium is the *gesamtkunstwerk*, the total work of art that incorporates all forms of art. This previously unexplored, holistic vision of the Left-Hand Path opens up exciting new frontiers on all levels and scales.

Many of us who are drawn to the Left-Hand Path carry a deep sense of being alien or a feeling of *sehnsucht* - a profound longing for a lost or forgotten homeland. Pandemonium explains why and provides a way home.

A CALL TO ACTION

Our words have brought us this far - only our actions can take us further. This is the Left-Hand Path. No gods or heroes will create this world for you. Or, rather, we ARE those Gods and Heroes. We are the Builders. Whatever tools of growth you have now (and we can provide more), whoever your closest intimates are right now (and others are out there), whatever space you have available in the present moment - you can begin building Pandemonium.

TODAY.

From there, it is just a matter of intensification and expansion. Become who you really are. Find the others. Fill your spaces with radical beauty and incandescent pleasure. That is why you are here. Reality is whatever you can get away with.

PANDEMONIUM IS Y-OURS.

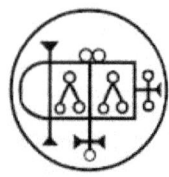

3

Liber AL vel Legis

Chapter I

NUIT

1. Had! The manifestation of Nuit.

Crowley identified Hadit (and Aiwaz) as Satan or Set numerous times throughout his works. The word "prince" in the title Prince of Darkness means "chief" or "first" (from *primus* - prime), and just as an exclamation of the name is the first word in this Book, Hadit is Prince to Nuit, who is ultimately metaphysical Darkness. Knowing this also further sets up our understanding of the next verse.

On a more mundane level - though it seems wrong to refer to it as such - our physics tells us that a perceiver or observer is necessary to the manifestation of reality. That very word "manifestation" appears in this first verse as well as in the last, and it is the esssential magical theme of this chapter.

Nuit is Darkness but also Space. The spelling of Her name (Nut) as "Nuit" creates a further similiarity to the name of the goddess Nit when spelled "Neith". Indeed, Nuit may be seen as only an aspect of Neith, who combines both the night and daytime skies within a greater concept of Space that matches Crowley's descriptions of Nuit as the total realm of all that is and all possibility. Neith is a very ancient goddess and in Her anthropomorphic form is both an archer and a weaver, both of which are symbolically very resonant with the practice of Magic.

In his book *Hecate's Fountain*, Kenneth Grant provides a looser commentary of his own upon this Book, and he lists several other particular manifestations of Nuit. Within the night sky in general, he focuses in upon the constellation of Ursa Major (which he calls Typhon) in particular. This may be a survival of those ancient days when Draco was the central constellation before being replaced by Ursa Major. For Grant, this is Darkness as the Primal Mother. To the Egyptians, Ursa Major was the constellation of the Thigh (of a bull), which was a symbol of Inheritance.

Crowley, in his New Comment for verse 24, compares Nuit to a Dragon and says:

"The Dragon in current symbolism refers to the North or Hollow of Heaven; thus to the Womb of Space, which is the container and breeder of all that exists."

The dwelling-place of Set was considered to be behind or beyond that central constellation, and there are related attributions in a number of other mythologies that concur in making this the special place of the Prince of Darkness.

Grant also lists the Moon and Woman as manifestations of Nuit, and these are elaborated upon in both symbolic and practical commentary throughout this chapter.

2. The unveiling of the company of heaven.

This verse is quite charged when one remembers that "unveiling" or revelation is the actual meaning of the misunderstood word "apocalypse", and that what is revealed here is knowledge that is meant to both destroy the old world through fire and establish a new one in its place.

Grant calls Hadit (as Set) the Son of the Primal Mother. He opens the Womb of Space by His birth, which opens the way for others like Him to come forth. As the First (Prince), he is the archetype and prototype of those others. *Xepera Xeper Xeperu*.

"Heaven" is that realm behind or beyond the stars of Nuit. It is also "Hell", the hidden or concealed place. This is what we mean by Pandemonium in its essential sense. It is the realm of the Daemons, who are like their brother and progenitor.

The nature of this realm can begin to be understood by contemplating what Crowley called his Star-Sponge Vision:

"I was on a retirement in a cottage overlooking Lake Pasquaney in New Hampshire. I lost consciousness of everything but a universal space in which were innumerable bright points, and I realized this as a physical representation of the universe, in what I may call its essential structure. I exclaimed, 'Nothingness with twinkles!' I concentrated upon this vision, with the result that the void space which had been the principal element of it diminished in importance; space appeared to be ablaze, yet the radiant points were not confused, and I thereupon completed my sentence with the exclamation, 'but what twinkles!'

"The next stage of this vision led to an identification of the blazing points with the stars of the firmament, with ideas, souls, etc. I perceived also that each star was connected by a ray of light with each other star. In the world of ideas each thought possessed a necessary relation with each other thought; each such relation is of course a thought in itself; each such ray is itself a star. It is here that the logical difficulty first presents itself. The seer has a direct perception of infinite series. Logically, therefore, it would appear as if the entire space must be filled up with a homogeneous blaze of light. This however is not the case. The space is completely full and yet the monads which fill it are perfectly distinct. The ordinary reader might well exclaim that such statements exhibit symptoms of mental confusion."

3. Every man and every woman is a star.

These "stars" are the monadic essence of sapient Entity, as will be discussed further below. The "unveiling of the company of heaven" by this verse, then, is the revelation that men and women are in truth these Daemons described above. This revelation is the Apocalypse that burns away the old world and establishes the new one in its place. The Constellation of the Thigh is the cosmic sigil of our Inheritance.

With regard to the process of Initiation, what we call the Daemon is what Crowley (after Abramelin) called the Holy Guardian Angel ("angel" means "messenger"). To know and converse with this Angel allows it to inform and teach the man or woman to remember their true essence and to Become something more than they were in their amnesia, to do more and to live more fully, all in accord with their truer and more vital essence.

The Daemons are the true Secret Chiefs and Hidden Masters, the true Great Old Ones coming forth into this universe to establish (resume) their reign.

4. Every number is infinite; there is no difference.

It is certainly true that a billion is no closer to the infinite than a dozen. Also, when we consider numbers as occult or twilight language symbols, they are more representative of qualities than of quantities. In the context of this verse's placement, these two ideas seem representative of required shifts in perspective for the audience described in the next verse to more fully appreciate this chapter.

5. Help me, o warrior lord of Thebes, in my unveiling before the Children of men!

For Crowley, this was addressed to himself identified with Ankh-f-n-khonsu, but Michael Aquino and Don Webb connect it to Amon and Montu respectively. As He became unpopular, the cult of Set was primarily absorbed into the cults of Amon and Montu. This verse can actually be taken as both a personal appeal to the reader (as for Crowley) and to the Prince of Darkness. As the Daemon or Angel can inform or inspire the Initiate, the Prince of Darkness can also do so both directly and by serving as an exemplar. The Constellation of the Thigh, recall, is the sign of Inheritance.

This dual interpretation leads directly into that of the next verse.

6. Be thou Hadit, my secret centre, my heart & my tongue!

Hadit is Prince to Nuit. The reader who wants to take up actual work with this material is to Become as the Prince of Darkness. Crowley took this verse solely to himself as scribe and Prophet of the Book, but now the reader would benefit from adopting this instruction as a personal practice. This is the point where the Book first becomes actionable.

Metaphysically, the entirety of the Second Chapter of this Book may be inserted here as Initiatory guidance and training that helps to prepare and empower the Company of Heaven - the Daemons - to more effectively perform and appreciate the Worship and Magic described through the rest of this chapter.

Using discernment and inspiration as provided by this commentary (in general) to guide you, Crowley's *Liber DLV* provides some basic ideas along these lines and the commentary on the Second Chapter (specifically) will provide many more.

7. Behold! it is revealed by Aiwass the minister of Hoor-paar-kraat.

For Crowley, Hoor-paar-kraat is an emblem of the Holy Guardian Angel or Daemon and he claimed Aiwass (or Aiwaz) as his own Angel. Moreover, Hoor-paar-kraat is the force behind Ra-hoor-khuit. Crowley adds that He has everything within Himself, but unmanifested. We can see Hoor-paar-kraat as a form of Hadit extended but unfulfilled.

As was pointed out in the beginning of this commentary, Crowley also repeatedly identified this god with Satan or Set. So, despite Hoor-paar-kraat being a form of Horus, Grant identifies Him with Set explicitly. The role of Set as a hidden presence and force within this Book and the roles of both Set and Horus as twin Aeonic forces are obviously also of central concern to Aquino and Webb in their commentaries. The subject will be resumed later in this commentary.

In any case, the existence of Aiwass as minister to Hoor-paar-kraat signals the beginning of the latter's extension or manifestation, as Aiwass is specifically referred to as a revealer.

8. The Khabs is in the Khu, not the Khu in the Khabs.

The Khabs is the 'star' or monadic essence of every man and woman. The Khu is the Psyche or Soul through which the Star experiences and comes into Being. To say that the Khabs is in the Khu rather than the other way around is to affirm that we are Divine at our core, rather than mere created souls existing within the light and grace of an external divinity.

Aquino comments that Khabs refers hieroglyphically to the gods of the astrological decans, a decan being a 10° division of the circle of the zodiac or night sky. Star Gods.

In the rituals of his Church of Satan, Anton LaVey employed frequent exclamation of the word "Shemhamforash!". This is a Hebrew word that means "The Explicit Name" and refers to a name for the monotheistic Hebrew deity that can be further divided (or explicated) into a cohort of 72 angels ruling these astrological decans. However, it seems unlikely that LaVey would be invoking Jehovah and his angels. It makes much more sense to consider that he took the name as one for Satan that also contained (by implication) an appeal to the corresponding 72 demons of the *Ars Goetia*. This would make the word an affirmation of the full complement of the assorted Powers of Darkness in one exuberant cheer.

The relationship of the demons in the *Ars Goetia* to the stellar decans provides a model for Pandemonium as the "company of heaven" where the Powers of Darkness are diversified, differentiated and expressed through a variety of distinct Beings. For this reason, we might even say that LaVey's use of "Shemhamforash" was simply an Aeonic placeholder for "Pandemonium" and that the latter would now be more appropriate for corresponding use in ritual. Concerning this, see also the comment to verse 20 below.

But to return to the basic message of the verse, the primary revelation that "every man and every woman is a star" has now become a description of spiritual anatomy, and this further sets up another practice in the next verse.

9. Worship then the Khabs, and behold my light shed over you!

Whose light, though? Is it Nuit or Aiwass speaking in this and the previous verse? This introduces the subject of the Black Light (see the comment to verse 60 below) or Black Flame.

The distinctly Left-Hand Path nature of this worship is again emphasized by Crowley's own superb statement in his New Comment: "The Khu in each of us includes the Cosmos as he knows it. To me, even another Khabs is only part of my Khu. Our own Khabs is our one sole Truth."

Aquino equates the Khu with the Black Light or Black Flame of Ipseity and Sapience, but we are following Crowley to equate it with the Psyche or Soul. This also calls for taking a side on the nature of Nuit, Herself. Aquino identifies Nuit with what he calls the Objective Universe, while Webb identifies Her with the Subjective Universe(s). Really, She would be both (all) of these, but it makes more sense to side with Webb in practice for a couple of reasons. First, we barely interact with any purely Objective Universe. This would be something like the quantum world or the mathematical realm of Pure Number. Second, as this Book puts its metaphysics down to the point-awareness of Hadit and the Otherness of Nuit, all of our actual subjective experience is left out if Nuit is defined simply as the Objective Universe. So it makes the most sense to focus on Nuit as the totality of our Experience.

There is another possible contradiction with the words of Hadit concerning worship in II:8 that is resolved if we understand the worship of the Khabs as simply identification with it or Self-realization as it. But all these considerations should be added to the practice called for under verse 6 above.

So, when we identify with the Khabs, the Black Flame as the light of Aiwass, Hoor-paar-kraat and Hadit flows through the Khu, nourishing it and being nourished by it. As Nuit is also the Moon to the Sun of Hadit, she reflects Black Light back to Him (again, see the comment to verse 60) as magical creativity and manifestations of that creativity. As some experiences contain more food or fuel for our Becoming than others, we discern a process of Initiation as cultivation of special forms of experience.

This may take some time to fully grasp. We must also remember that the Black Flame is a Mystery - the central Mystery of the Left-Hand Path - and that this Book was an imperfect revelation of things to come. Still, to wrestle with questions of the Black Flame directly strengthens the Black Flame within us.

10. Let my servants be few & secret: they shall rule the many & the known.

A reign not only of elite rulers but invisible ones - not just aristocracy, but cryptocracy. Yet Crowley wrote that not only is the Law for ALL, but Magick as well. As an actual political question, the solution to this apparent contradiction is resolved by Thomas Jefferson's "aristocracy of achievement arising out of a democracy of opportunity".

The service was outlined in verse 6.

11. These are fools that men adore; both their Gods & their men are fools.

12. Come forth, o children, under the stars, & take your fill of love!

This is foreshadowing of the ritual described in verse 61 below. Here, the important points are introduced. First, the stars may be the literal stars of the sky or (and) the metaphysical Daemonic Stars above us that we also are. Likewise, to take our fill of love may refer to forms of love in life or (and) to that spiritual love that exists among the Company of Heaven. Indeed, all our loves in life should contain and reflect that greater Love.

This is more than a ritual, though. It is a call to a much greater process. It is a call to "come forth" as those Daemons by placing ourselves under their tutelage and remanifesting that Love on Earth. Consider this in connection with verse 53.

The importance of Night and the night sky are emphasized even more strongly later in Aquino's *Book of Coming Forth by Night* (note the title in relation to this verse and verses 2 and 3), where it is said to speak to Set at night when the sky becomes an entrance and not a barrier. Those who are drawn to the Left-Hand Path are very often nocturnal by nature. There is more to this than symbolism.

13. I am above you and in you. My ecstasy is in yours. My joy is to see your joy.

This verse further substantiates the idea that we look to our experience of Nuit as being our Experience in general. It is where Self and Other, Hadit and Nuit, meet as one and is the co-creation of both. Any ecstasy or joy coming out of this meeting requires both. Nuit experiences nothing without an Experiencer, but will reflect an Experiencer as the Moon does the Sun.

All Beauty is Her flesh. All Pleasure is Her touch.

14. Above, the gemmèd azure is

   The naked splendour of Nuit;

She bends in ecstasy to kiss

> The secret ardours of Hadit.
>
> The wingèd globe, the starry blue,
>
> Are mine, O Ankh-af-na-khonsu!

This is Crowley's own poetry based on the so-called Stele of Revealing, the funeral stele of Ankh-f-n-khonsu. It is not part of the original dictation but does both recapitulate the previous verse and provide a link to the next, as it can refer to either the general metaphysics of the Book or a sexual ritual.

15. Now ye shall know that the chosen priest & apostle of infinite space is the prince-priest the Beast; and in his woman called the Scarlet Woman is all power given. They shall gather my children into their fold: they shall bring the glory of the stars into the hearts of men.

Space is the most important natural element to the Left-Hand Path because it is what allows for differences in viewpoint and thus separation and distinction. Without space, there would only be one viewpoint and nothing to view. The space introduced between Self and Other provides distinction and definition. The space between things facilitates differentiation between them.

Moreover, space provides the theater or arena for things to happen. For Crowley, space means possibility, so infinite space means infinite possibilities. Space is important to the Left-Hand Path in this sense, too, because it merges with the idea of metaphysical Darkness. This is the Darkness of Mystery and the Unmanifest, from which everything comes and from which anything *might* come (refer back to the quote in the comment for verse 1 above).

In their incarnate offices, the Beast and the Scarlet Woman have the tasks of creating spaces (of all kinds) for the Work to occur in and of providing Mystery to fuel it. Within those spaces and around those Mysteries, they can then evangelize, ritualize and so on as need be. The unveiling of the Company of Heaven is the message. Space and Mystery, however, are the foundations of their priestcraft.

16. For he is ever a sun, and she a moon. But to him is the winged secret flame, and to her the stooping starlight.

One one level, this is a simple repetition of things that have already been said, but then why waste the words? We might further consider all of the psychological and alchemical - even Surreal - symbolism of the Sun and Moon. Of course, with regard to Surrealism, Nuit would certainly embody the Super-Reality that it seeks, and (in relation to Hadit) the quest for the liberation of Desire as well.

17. But ye are not so chosen.

Here, a strictly personal note - I would consider myself the CHOOSER.

As a result, I take the most extreme Left-Hand Path stance to this Book as a whole, relating it as much to myself personally as Crowley and Aquino do in their commentaries - but actually even more so, because I am not considering my role in relation to the text but rather the role of the text in relation to me. As Pandemonium contains and connects the Aeons, all the Gods and Magic of each Aeon come to serve

Pandemonium.

18. Burn upon their brows, o splendrous serpent!

The power of Hadit in the form of the royal uraeus, the mark of the Masters from verse 10. In his comment, Aquino quotes from Utterance 683 in the Pyramid Texts: "This is the Uraeus which came forth from Set."

The Serpent symbolism in relation to Hadit is an important theme of the Second Chapter.

19. O azure-lidded woman, bend upon them!

The experience of Nuit's affections as a result of these practices.

20. The key of the rituals is in the secret word which I have given unto him.

For Crowley, this word was ABRAHADABRA and he wrote about it extensively. But we are going to put that aside, and I am going to give you

PANDEMONIUM

and briefly but clearly explain why it, in fact, is the certain and supreme key of the rituals.

Pandemonium is a Latinized Greek word that means "All-Daemon-Place". Its three parts refer to spiritual or psychic factors, social factors and environmental factors. Moreover, it unites all of these within itself. This is because these are not just three categories but three dimensions of a holistic continuum in which each dimension or dynamic affects the others.

Pandemonium refers to Initiatory growth of the Self and corresponding Magical improvements to social and environmental conditions, which then create and support further growth opportunities for the Self through feedback loops.

In this, it unites (reunites) and expands upon the meanings of Aeonic placeholders such as Abrahadabra and Shemhamforash (verse 8).

Though its manifest forms might look different for each of us, Pandemonium is the Deep Desire of EVERYONE and all Magic(k) ultimately aims toward it. As the continuum of Deep Desire, its manifestation is tied to the manifestation of Nuit. As well as defining aims, however, its three dimensions or categories of factors also provide the actual structure and substance of ritual design. Both in ritual and result, we use it to create a whole context or ecology of self-sustained transformation rather than just a single, unsupported condition or effect.

See also the comment to verse 60.

21. With the God & the Adorer I am nothing: they do not see me. They are as upon the earth; I am Heaven, and there is no other God than me, and my lord Hadit.

The Satanist and the Setian will be reminded of the Statement of Leviathan at the end of the *Diabolicon*, where only Leviathan and the Red Magus remain once everything else has been swept away. It is a tempting comparison and a strong case for it will be presented as we continue.

But along those lines, the use of the word "Heaven"

may hold a double meaning. The first refers to cosmic space as the theater of possibilities, the great arts studio of creation and manifestation. Relatedly, though, we might also think of Heaven in its more colloqiual sense as a place of ultimate happiness and pleasure. This is what Nuit might be for those who master Her Magic(k).

To see and know Nuit, Crowley's *Liber XI* has some good practices to begin with, again with the discernment and inspiration gained here to guide you.

22. Now, therefore, I am known to ye by my name Nuit, and to him by a secret name which I will give him when at last he knoweth me. Since I am Infinite Space, and the Infinite Stars thereof, do ye also thus. Bind nothing! Let there be no difference made among you between any one thing & any other thing; for thereby there cometh hurt.

"Bind nothing!" - The Gods of this Book proclaim GROWTH, the growth and development of all things according to their own nature within the infinite possibilities of infinite space.

"no difference" - Nuit contains all perspectives and the possibility of all experiences. Hadit can hold only one position or viewpoint at a time. Learning to be able to shift or hold those positions at will is important training.

These are two important keys to the Magic(k) of Nuit, which is Manifestation. In the process, we will each come to know Nuit in our own way (Her "secret name" with us).

23. But whoso availeth in this, let him be the chief of

all!

"Chief", again, being a meaning of "Prince" - the Master Magican per the previous verse.

The Left-Hand Path Initiate is constantly confronted by his experience of the universe in the form of something often referred to as the Abyss. The Crossing of this Abyss is an Ordeal associated with the state of Being called Master of the Temple. This Abyss is usually painted as one enormous thing, an ontological and metaphysical Grand Canyon blown up a thousand times bigger and there to be faced and crossed (or not) by the advanced Initiate in a great Ordeal to attain the Other Side. This is not entirely accurate. It actually winds and twists through your whole life from the time you are born. Sometimes it is only as wide as a ribbon. Sometimes it is as thin as a thread. We cross it in every single moment of decision where we choose honesty over fraud, responsibility over resignation and power over weakness.

What happens is that if you make enough small crossings, you will be led to bigger, more profound and more difficult crossings. If you cross enough of those, you will be led to something so deep within you, so fundamental to you, that it constitutes a Crossing that entirely alters your relationship to the universe, reality, the Dream - whatever you want to call it. You have passed Beyond.

But this relation to Nuit becomes most perfect in the state called Ipsissimus. In his *Liber B vel Magi*, Crowley advises "contemplat[ing] each in turn, raising it to the ultimate power of Infinity. Wherein Sorrow is Joy, and Change is Stability, and Selflessness is Self."

My own comment upon that verse (16) explains:

"For the Left-Hand Path's Master of the Temple, any human Sorrow in the face of the absolute Isolation of the Self evaporates into Joy as that Isolation is fully Understood in terms of Freedom.

"For the Magus, Change becomes Stability when the Word of Laozi is Understood: that a web of dynamic yet equilibriating forces creates resilience. With regard to himself, the Magus may simply realize that one stays upright on a bicycle by continuing to move forward.

"For the Ipsissimus, Selflessness becomes Self when both the Freedom of the Master and the Magus' relation to the forces of stability-in-change become thorough, perfected and integrated. In casting off all former identifications and relations that amounted to a false and limiting sense of being, the Ipsissimus becomes nothing but his own true Self. By mastering the play of elements and forces through the expression (and exteriorization) of his Word as a Magus, the Ipsissimus remanifests that Self and is free to act in pan-determinism as he wills."

24. I am Nuit, and my word is six and fifty.

25. Divide, add, multiply, and understand.

26. Then saith the prophet and slave of the beauteous one: Who am I, and what shall be the sign? So she answered him, bending down, a lambent flame of blue, all-touching, all penetrant, her lovely hands upon the black earth, & her lithe body arched for love, and her soft feet not hurting the little flowers: Thou knowest! And the sign shall be my ecstasy, the consciousness of the continuity of existence, the omnipresence of my body.

The Black Earth remanifests the Black Flame.

See the comment to verse 60.

Ecstasy is the sign. Passion, meaning, engagement, pleasure, flow.

It is worth noting that "the omnipresence of my body" is not the original dictation, which was "'the unfragmentary non-atomic fact of my universality". Crowley asked for permission to change it because he thought it made no sense. The original phrase and Hadit's words in II:3, when combined, are suggestive of the holographic universe proposed by David Bohm.

In that Her feet are upon the "little flowers" and Her "lovely hands upon the black earth", a process of Manifestation is suggested by Her very pose.

27. Then the priest answered & said unto the Queen of Space, kissing her lovely brows, and the dew of her light bathing his whole body in a sweet-smelling perfume of sweat: O Nuit, continuous one of Heaven, let it be ever thus; that men speak not of Thee as One but as None; and let them speak not of thee at all, since thou art continuous!

28. None, breathed the light, faint & færy, of the stars, and two.

29. For I am divided for love's sake, for the chance of union.

As both Darkness and Infinite Space, Nuit is both None and All.

This is a good place to return to Neith and her activity

as a weaver.

This book can not be simply viewed as either a scripture or a grimoire alone, but is best understood as a *tantra* - which is to say, in a sense, both. This Sanskrit term refers to a loom or weaving. Metaphorically, then, it has also come to refer to a text, a system of practice, a ritual, a magical spell or sexual intercourse, as these are all 'weavings'. And this Book, of course, is a weaving of all of these weavings.

30. This is the creation of the world, that the pain of division is as nothing, and the joy of dissolution all.

31. For these fools of men and their woes care not thou at all! They feel little; what is, is balanced by weak joys; but ye are my chosen ones.

Another reminder that this is most emphatically an elitist system. Desire and force of passion are keys, and such talk foreshadows the spirit of Hadit in the Second Chapter, most directly verse II:18.

32. Obey my prophet! follow out the ordeals of my knowledge! seek me only! Then the joys of my love will redeem ye from all pain. This is so: I swear it by the vault of my body; by my sacred heart and tongue; by all I can give, by all I desire of ye all.

33. Then the priest fell into a deep trance or swoon, & said unto the Queen of Heaven; Write unto us the ordeals; write unto us the rituals; write unto us the law!

34. But she said: the ordeals I write not: the rituals shall be half known and half concealed: the Law is for all.

35. This that thou writest is the threefold book of Law.

36. My scribe Ankh-af-na-khonsu, the priest of the princes, shall not in one letter change this book; but lest there be folly, he shall comment thereupon by the wisdom of Ra-Hoor-Khu-it.

Permission was given for the change to verse 26 above, but there are other issues in this area that will be addressed as they come up. For the saddest example, see the comment to III:37.

37. Also the mantras and spells; the obeah and the wanga; the work of the wand and the work of the sword; these he shall learn and teach.

Crowley seems to have taken "the obeah and the wanga" somewhat poetically, but may have been aware of the book *Obeah Simplified - The True Wanga* by Prof. Myal Djumboh Cassecanarie (1895 EV). If the verse refers Crowley to that book specifically, not taking the phrase more literally might be considered a lapse.

As he admits in his New Comment: "This...includes raising the dead, bewitching cattle, making rain, acquiring goods, fascinating judges, and all the rest of the programme."

If we are looking at this Book as a tantra, the prominent role of material sorcery and 'low magic' is quite traditional to that classification.

However, Crowley's definition, postulate and theorems of Magick (given in his *Magick in Theory and Practice*) that align all thought, word and deed into magical activity are also very important and helpful in fulfilling the instructions of verse 6.

It is also noteworthy here that Anton LaVey's three rituals in *The Satanic Bible* correspond to the three chapters of this Book, and that those Conjurations can provide focus and keys to operant manifestation of things described more abstractly in this text. The metaphysical may be translated into the very physical.

Crowley notes that only the wand and the sword are mentioned, but not the cup or disk. The wand and the sword refer to the dual force of Set and Horus, respectively. That will be covered more fully in the commentary to the Third Chapter, as will the role of the disk. The cup is certainly relevant to most of this chapter without real need to be mentioned explicitly. Nonetheless, I will devote an appended essay to both the cup and the disk.

38. He must teach; but he may make severe the ordeals.

Be aware that the ordeals are personal - even karmic - and not mere ceremonies.

39. The word of the Law is Θελημα.

An important precursor to Crowley's system can be found in the fictional, counter-monastic Abbey of Thélème described by the 16th-century French writer Francois Rabelais. Of the Thélèmites, it is written:

"All their life was spent not in laws, statutes, or rules, but according to their own free will and pleasure. They rose out of their beds when they thought good; they did eat, drink, labour, sleep, when they had a mind to it and were disposed

for it. None did awake them, none did offer to constrain them to eat, drink, nor to do any other thing; for so had Gargantua established it. In all their rule and strictest tie of their order there was but this one clause to be observed,

"Do What Thou Wilt..."

This sort of thing was attempted on a grand and visionary (if flawed) scale by Charles Fourier. Crowley, of course, briefly ran his own Abbey of Thelema in Sicily. Even if unsuccesful, these were important experiments in the context of Pandemonium because they were actual worlds. They manifested the full continuum of psychic, social and environmental dimensions.

The general meaning of *Thelema* is Will, as anyone reading this probably knows. Crowley thought of it in terms of harmony between will and action. Integrity. However, it does not simply refer to disciplined willpower (important as that is) but also to a wish or desire.

Will implies Selfhood, which reaffirms the true Left-Hand Path nature of Thelema's proper expression. The Self experiences itself most purely *as* a Self when it acts according to its own agency and volition against the inertia of its environment, society or its own habits.

Desire is highly relevant to the subject of Nuit, It is the reach that exceeds one's grasp and employs willed effort in the manifestation of new possibilities.

Desire and its fulfillment - LaVey's *Indulgence* - give us our Why in life. Will or *Thelema*, then, is the means or the How. Aquino's *Xeper* - the process of Becoming - is the ultimate result and the ultimate Indulgence of the Self. It provides the What of existence, the drive of Sapience for endless expansion. When these are applied in a balanced and holistic way to all the dimensions of existence, the result is Pandemonium, the Kingdom.

40. Who calls us Thelemites will do no wrong, if he look but close into the word. For there are therein Three Grades, the Hermit, and the Lover, and the man of Earth. Do what thou wilt shall be the whole of the Law.

It is interesting that these three grades - in the order given - reflect the model for a rite of passage as explained by the ethnographer Arnold van Gennep. In this model, the initiate is first separated in some way from his or her familiar world. Then, in a liminal state, the initiate undergoes an experience and/or learns information that changes them dramatically. Finally, the initiate is reintegrated into the world but within a new mode of life.

The Left-Hand Path usually begins with antinomian acts of rebellion against cultural traditions and social rules. The deeper form is rebellion against one's own habitual and unconscious traditions and rules. This leads into the middle stage where the Initiate learns about who they really are and what they really want, along with building some skills for enhancing the former and acquiring the latter. Because the Left-Hand Path is thoroughly worldly, this flows right into the final stage of reintegration and application. Failure on the Path most commonly manifests as remaining permanently stuck in the first stage of superficial rebellion.

Crowley applied the three grades from this verse in the opposite order, however, which does not seem to have been very successful. To bring van Gennep's model, the standard Left-Hand Path approach and the actual instructions of this Book back into proper alignment, the Initiate should begin as a Hermit, working to become Hadit as instructed in verse 6 above. Next, as a Lover, the Worship and Magic of Nuit should be mastered. Then the (Wo)Man of the Earth comes forth as one of the Kings described throughout the text, to wage war and take Dominion.

While Initiation is never a linear process in actual practice, this general order can be seen to be more correct. This system also aligns with the three dimensions of Pandemonium, bolstering my assertion in the comment to verse 20 above.

Note also how the structures of both ABRA-HAD-ABRA and PAN-DEMON-IUM additionally correspond to the structure of this Book, with the components of the latter more explicitly expressing the specific manifestations of the general extension expressed by the former. Consider the esoteric link to Revelation 16:13 with regard to the Book, formulae and grades, as well.

41. The word of Sin is Restriction. O man! refuse not thy wife, if she will! O lover, if thou wilt, depart! There is no bond that can unite the divided but love: all else is a curse. Accursèd! Accursèd be it to the æons! Hell.

Again, "Bind nothing!"

42. Let it be that state of manyhood bound and

loathing. So with thy all; thou hast no right but to do thy will.

Crowley's opinion was that a Magician must have attained the Knowledge and Conversation of their Holy Guardian Angel (Daemon) before any real Magic(k) could be done. To put it as simply as possible, you need to know who you are and what you want in order to most effectively go out and get it. It is about Integrity in the most essential sense of the word. The ordinary person has a number of weak desires and intentions going off in different directions. Their attention and energies, then, are scattered and pitted against each other. But for someone that has begun to know who they really are and tamed those energies (see the comment for verse 44 below), the way forward is much more clear.

43. Do that, and no other shall say nay.

44. For pure will, unassuaged of purpose, delivered from the lust of result, is every way perfect.

This verse highlights the difference between common willpower and the Thelemic Will, which includes willpower but is something greater. We know that our conscious awareness is only a small part of our total mind. Most of our intentions and decisions come from the subconscious or unconscious.

The bulk of our work is in using our conscious willpower to expose and resolve complexes in the deeper mind and to strengthen its Integrity. As this work is done, our Will flows ever more strongly and directly.

Remember that Neith is an archer, and we might say

that She is a Zen archer.

45. The Perfect and the Perfect are one Perfect and not two; nay, are none!

46. Nothing is a secret key of this law. Sixty-one the Jews call it; I call it eight, eighty, four hundred & eighteen.

47. But they have the half: unite by thine art so that all disappear.

48. My prophet is a fool with his one, one, one; are not they the Ox, and none by the Book?

49. Abrogate are all rituals, all ordeals, all words and signs. Ra-Hoor-Khuit hath taken his seat in the East at the Equinox of the Gods; and let Asar be with Isa, who also are one. But they are not of me. Let Asar be the adorant, Isa the sufferer; Hoor in his secret name and splendour is the Lord initiating.

Crowley wrote extensively about the shift in tropes, themes and formulae attending the change of Aeon as he perceived it, the only comment left to make is that he did not go far enough. More on that in the comment to II:5.

"Hoor" is Hoor-paar-kraat and His role as "the Lord initiating" is explained in verse 6 above and the entirety of the Second Chapter. And again, it is implied throughout the Book that the "secret name" is Set, though this may also apply to the unique and personal Daemon of each man and woman.

50. There is a word to say about the Hierophantic task. Behold! there are three ordeals in one, and it

may be given in three ways. The gross must pass through fire; let the fine be tried in intellect, and the lofty chosen ones in the highest. Thus ye have star & star, system & system; let not one know well the other!

The Path of Becoming is necessarily as diverse and varied as those who walk it.

Pandemonium may be made in some way explicable and applicable to all Aeons, all cultures, all societies and all persons.

51. There are four gates to one palace; the floor of that palace is of silver and gold; lapis lazuli & jasper are there; and all rare scents; jasmine & rose, and the emblems of death. Let him enter in turn or at once the four gates; let him stand on the floor of the palace. Will he not sink? Amn. Ho! warrior, if thy servant sink? But there are means and means. Be goodly therefore: dress ye all in fine apparel; eat rich foods and drink sweet wines and wines that foam! Also, take your fill and will of love as ye will, when, where and with whom ye will! But always unto me.

Here, I agree with Webb that this palace should be interpreted as our own Being. While such a physical environment might be built - perhaps as an alternative to the Golden Dawn's Vault of the Adepti - and would be spectacular, more benefit is to be gained from taking it as an allegory of the microcosm.

The four gates, then, are the Physical, Emotional, Intellectual and Daemonic aspects of Being. In Initiation, these may certainly be worked with in turn or all at once. Crowley says that lapis lazuli corresponds to Nuit and jasper corresponds to Hadit, as would silver and gold if the couple are considered as Moon and Sun. He also says that jasmine (white) and rose (red) correspond to sacraments. The presence of the emblems of death is strange in light of verse 49, but less so when the palace is taken as our own being or our sphere of life. Crowley seems to support this view, himself, in the one example of the rare scents, which he tentatively identifies with states of consciousness.

As Magicians and practitioners of a Left-Hand Path tantra, all of the wealth, beauty and pleasures listed in the second half of the verse are not only appropriate to our palace but are sacraments and our birthright. We can easily imagine Anton LaVey smiling and nodding at all of this, the celebration of Indulgence on all levels. In developing our practice, the Hindu cult of Lakshmi and the yoga of Padmini Vidya are inspirational.

For the last sentence, see the next verse.

52. If this be not aright; if ye confound the space-marks, saying: They are one; or saying, They are many; if the ritual be not ever unto me: then expect the direful judgments of Ra Hoor Khuit!

This seems to be the most appropriate place to talk about Crowley's advocacy of Sex Magick - for which he is perhaps most widely known - as Nuit is calling us here to its ultimate form.

This term can actually be applied to four types of activity. The most abstract of these would be the illustration of an alchemical *hierogamos* ("sacred marriage") between the Male and Female principles or archetypes. This might be more properly referred to as Sex Mysticism, though it may provide a context for the other forms (as it does in this Book).

The most immediately practical application of Sex Magick is the use of orgasm as an amplifier of whatever aim or focus is held firmly in the mind at the climactic moment. This is often best employed as a solo operation.

Between these, a more extended project is the exploration of sexuality and Deep Desire as a form of increasing Self-knowledge and in nourishing or transcending aspects of the persona or character as willed. These activities may be pursued outside of the strictly archetypal Male-Female *hierogamos* - as they certainly were by Crowley, himself.

These three types of Sex Magick could all be classed as Sex-as-Magick, while the fourth would be more accurately classed as Magic(k)-as-Sex. This Mystery is rarely explored, though it is the main point of this chapter in this Book. Here, the Magician's operations and experiences may be seen as a form of sexual intercourse between him- or her-Self and the continuum of Everything Else personified as a lover: Nuit.

This perspective can also unite and add new depth to the other three Sex Magick forms as well as to all magical operations not involving sexuality in any literal way. Refer back to verse 20 where PANDEMONIUM is explained as the supreme key to the rituals and combine that understanding with our understanding of Nuit as our Experience. This is how we align everything and obey Her call that the ritual be ever unto Her.

A Left-Hand *bhakti* or devotional yoga may seem like a contradiction to some, but this is how we do it: as intercourse, exchange, dialogue - not union.

In the Third Chapter, we will see Ra-hoor-khuit as punisher of Right-Hand Path doctrines and devotions. Nuit warns us that we should have nought to do with them.

53. This shall regenerate the world, the little world my sister, my heart & my tongue, unto whom I send this kiss. Also, o scribe and prophet, though thou be of the princes, it shall not assuage thee nor absolve thee. But ecstasy be thine and joy of earth: ever To me! To me!

It would probably be a leap for most people to understand the Apocalypse (verses 1-3) as healing, but all of this should show how it is exactly so. It brings truths out from lies, and harmony from confusion. The apocalyptic manifestation of Pandemonium is, precisely, the regeneration of the world.

The Setian proclaims: "As Earth in Space, I am Become!" - comparable to Fire in Darkness or Water in the Desert.

The world is like Nuit, a theater or arena of possibility. A place of space, energy, matter and time. But it holds the potential for more and greater possibilities than empty space. It is a place of manifestation; and through the work described here, it is transformed. Like Hadit, and like us, it also becomes the heart and tongue of Nuit.

The Black Earth remanifests the Black Flame.

See also the comment for verse 57 below.

54. Change not as much as the style of a letter; for behold! thou, o prophet, shalt not behold all these mysteries hidden therein.

Again, wait until you see the tragedy of III:37.

55. The child of thy bowels, he shall behold them.

56. Expect him not from the East, nor from the West; for from no expected house cometh that child. Aum! All words are sacred and all prophets true; save only that they understand a little; solve the first half of the equation, leave the second unattacked. But thou hast all in the clear light, and some, though not all, in the dark.

57. Invoke me under my stars! Love is the law, love under will. Nor let the fools mistake love; for there are love and love. There is the dove, and there is the serpent. Choose ye well! He, my prophet, hath chosen, knowing the law of the fortress, and the great mystery of the House of God.

All these old letters of my Book are aright; but צ is not the Star. This also is secret: my prophet shall reveal it to the wise.

Once more, "stars" has the same double meaning, literal and metaphorical. It may mean under the night sky, it may mean in view of Ursa Major in particular, it may simply mean at night (even if indoors), but it definitely means under the spiritual constellations expressed in the Star-Sponge Vision. We might say that invoking under the stars in a literal sense (outdoors) might be optional, but invoking under that Company of Stars (the Daemons) is always mandatory.

Concerning the office of Scarlet Woman or Priestess, refer back to the comment for verse 1 and the idea of Woman as a symbol or manifestation of Nuit. Applied in ritual, this is the deeper meaning to be found in the Satanic tradition of a nude woman acting as a living altar, underlying the more palpable aesthetic and erotic stimulation that she produces in the participants.

Viewed through an inderstanding of Pandemonium, this living altar functions as a bridge between realms. The woman is, herself, a Star or Daemon and her female body is symbolic of the continuum of experience represented by Nuit - a land of milk and honey, as the saying goes - and the materiality of her body makes it like a talisman anchoring the one realm to the other, uniting them within herself.

Whether she is nude or not, and whatever she is doing, this is the primary consideration and understanding.

In Christianity, the Dove and Serpent are traditionally associated with Christ and Satan, respectively. However, in some forms of Gnosticism, the Serpent is also representative of Christ - or rather, it is specifically the Serpent of Eden who returns *as* the Christ. In the Bible, Jesus advises his followers to be BOTH wise as serpents and gentle as doves.

We can use these references to interpret the verse in a

couple of different ways. First, for the most part, the Love described in this Book is not gentle in the usual weakened sense that the word connotes. Moreover, choosing well would mean to choose *wisely*. And as we will see, Hadit identifies with the Serpent explicitly in His chapter. But in any given moment, we may also choose as we will for that moment, as our own discretion guides. Love under Will.

In whatever case, we should always be aware that our Love is a multiplying force. It magnifies and nourishes whatever we direct it to.

Concerning the House of God, this refers to personally antinomian acts that may be represented by the Tower card of the Tarot. There is also an entirely other sense of the House of God expressed throughout the Third Chapter and its commentary. The two are complementary but should not be confused.

58. I give unimaginable joys on earth: certainty, not faith, while in life, upon death; peace unutterable, rest, ecstasy; nor do I demand aught in sacrifice.

59. My incense is of resinous woods & gums; and there is no blood therein: because of my hair the trees of Eternity.

Crowley relates "trees of Eternity" to the World-Tree (or Cosmos-Tree), a common symbol of the organic World-Order in many cultures, deriving from the Proto-Indo-European concept of the *Xartus*.

He also describes trees or wood as symbolic of growth, which is the meaning of Wood as an element among the Chinese. Blood, while it has other important symbolism, here partakes too much of death.

It would make sense for the resinous woods and gums to correspond to the Moon or perhaps even the stars of Ursa Major.

60. My number is 11, as all their numbers who are of us. The Five Pointed Star, with a Circle in the Middle, & the circle is Red. My colour is black to the blind, but the blue & gold are seen of the seeing. Also I have a secret glory for them that love me.

The occult significance of 11 is as the number of Magic(k) and sorcery. Like Crowley's ABRAHADABRA, there are also 11 letters in PANDEMONIUM. The phrase "as all their numbers who are of us" highlights the link by indicating that others exist - the "company of heaven" - as Pandemonium is the Abode of all Daemons,

Grant presents the Pentagram as a sign of Woman (and Nuit) in what he and others call its 'averse' form, but we know that this is actually its proper and original form as constructed from the pentagon. In this original form, before being reversed to the more static and 'acceptable' form and accruing varieties of superflous symbolism, it was a simple expression of Perfection, partaking of the golden ratio (phi). It is this original, single-point-down form that should be used in the creation of the Seal (or yantra) of Nuit. There was confusion regarding the Star in the dictation and Crowley never did quite get it right. As Set clarifies in the *Book of Coming Forth by Night*:

"When I first came to this world, I gave to you my great pentagram, timeless measure of beauty through proportion.

And it was shown inverse, that creation and change be exalted above rest and preservation."

Nuit's color is black to the blind because she is Darkness and the common people can see nothing within Her. But to Her own true Children, the wonders and possibilities within Her are radiant. Our unfolding Work is their Manifestation.

As Milton put it: "...yet from those flames no light, but rather darkness visible..."

Specifically, blue becomes the color of Nuit, Herself, and gold is the color of Ra-Hoor-Khut as Her Child manifesting within and through Her. Concerning the latter, note the spelling and see also the comments for III:1, 21 and 38.

61. But to love me is better than all things: if under the night stars in the desert thou presently burnest mine incense before me, invoking me with a pure heart, and the Serpent flame therein, thou shalt come a little to lie in my bosom. For one kiss wilt thou then be willing to give all; but whoso gives one particle of dust shall lose all in that hour. Ye shall gather goods and store of women and spices; ye shall wear rich jewels; ye shall exceed the nations of the earth in splendour & pride; but always in the love of me, and so shall ye come to my joy. I charge you earnestly to come before me in a single robe, and covered with a rich headdress. I love you! I yearn to you! Pale or purple, veiled or voluptuous, I who am all pleasure and purple, and drunkenness of the innermost sense, desire you. Put on the wings, and arouse the coiled splendour within you: come unto me!

Another description of the same ritual. The Serpent flame is that of Hadit, fully described in His chapter.

She wants no sacrifice, once again highlighting the true Left-Hand Path nature of this tantra. She tells us to approach Her like we should approach any Woman - as a proper lover, not a supplicant.

And, once again, we hear about all the great and tangible wealth and beauty that will accrue to us as a result of this practice.

62. At all my meetings with you shall the priestess say—and her eyes shall burn with desire as she stands bare and rejoicing in my secret temple—To me! To me! calling forth the flame of the hearts of all in her love-chant.

63. Sing the rapturous love-song unto me! Burn to me perfumes! Wear to me jewels! Drink to me, for I love you! I love you!

64. I am the blue-lidded daughter of Sunset; I am the naked brilliance of the voluptuous night-sky.

65. To me! To me!

66. The Manifestation of Nuit is at an end.

In summary, this chapter presents a body (!) of related teachings, rituals and practices (forming a *tantra*) based upon the ultimate form of Sexual Magic(k). In this Magic(k), the total Experience of the Magician is seen as a single, holistic Other and as a Lover - THE Lover. The continuing intercourse between them is experienced as completely romantic and erotic in nature, and the relationship provides the matrix or context of ongoing expansion of Being and Becoming.

4

Liber AL vel Legis

Chapter II

HADIT

1. Nu! the hiding of Hadit.

There are two things to be aware of with this phrase. First, we can liken Hadit to the seed concealed within the womb of His bride, Nuit. His (re)birth in turn reveals and manifests Nuit as described in the previous chapter. The other side to this, though, is the problem of Hadit as the Self becoming obscured by identifications with various phenomena within Nuit. This issue and the hurt that comes of it will be repeatedly brought up in this chapter.

2. Come! all ye, and learn the secret that hath not yet been revealed. I, Hadit, am the complement of Nu, my bride. I am not extended, and Khabs is the name of my House.

But away from hiding and back to revelation. This chapter is the book of Hadit and represents His birth and the birth of those like Him, the Company of Heaven - the Daemons - as described in I:1-3, 5-6 (see those comments).

As we might have previously surmised, the Khabs is the part of our spiritual anatomy that corresponds to Hadit but it is made explicit here. Likewise, we can assume the Khu to be the complementary part of our spiritual anatomy that corresponds to Nuit.

Hadit is not extended, He is absolutely Isolate. See verse 23.

3. In the sphere I am everywhere the centre, as she, the circumference, is nowhere found.

Every Self is the center of its own world. Meanwhile, Darkness as Mystery or potential has no end or limit.

Remember also the comment to I:26.

4. Yet she shall be known & I never.

See the opening verses of both this chapter and the First. As the saying goes, the eye can not see itself.

In the Psychosynthesis teachings of Roberto Assagioli, the process of Dis-Identification is of fundamental importance. It is recognized that our thoughts, emotions, body and roles in life are all things that we HAVE, not things that we ARE. We, ourselves, are simply a point of awareness and intention.

Around this point, these other things may be added to, subtracted from or altered - but anything that you can perceive is not you. You are the Subject and they are the Object. Dis-Identification is the process of dissolving identifications with these objects of awareness.

Below, Hadit refers to Himself as a Snake. One aspect

of this symbolism refers to His extension through experience of various identities, mindsets, roles, relationships and environments, but it must be remembered that all of these are also merely 'skins' that may be shed at will in an ongoing process of Becoming and renewal.

5. Behold! the rituals of the old time are black. Let the evil ones be cast away; let the good ones be purged by the prophet! Then shall this Knowledge go aright.

This is an area where Crowley failed grotesquely by using far too light a hand. Everything Abrahamic should have been swept away entirely, including such claptrap as the qabala. Imagine what he might have done with all the free time and attention - and how much more clear and tidy his work might have been - had he followed through on this instruction.

This is of even greater import when we consider the capitalization of "Knowledge" in this verse as a reference to *Gnosis*. Crowley tried to revive Gnosticism within Thelema but does not seem to have understood it very well (though to be fair, the Nag Hammadi treasure hoard of Gnostic texts had not been discovered yet). The God of Abraham, YHVH or Jehovah, is considered to be a monstrous demiurge - not unlike the Choronzon of the Enochian system - and far removed from anything healthy or beneficial to the Soul.

Regardless, a powerful Gnostic stream comes forth in this chapter, beginning with the very next verse.

6. I am the flame that burns in every heart of man,

and in the core of every star. I am Life, and the giver of Life, yet therefore is the knowledge of me the knowledge of death.

The capitalization of "Life" indicates Daemonic Life rather than mere biological life. In Greek, this is ZOE. Crowley thought that the Word of Jesus Christ as a Magus was Agape, but we can now easily show that it would have been Zoe. Consider the second part of John 10:10 - "I am come that they might have life, and that they might have it more abundantly." - and that most of Jesus' miracles were healings and resurrections. Even the turning of water into wine ties into this if we consider it esoterically - "The Blood is the Life."

Furthermore, the Gospel of Thomas is replete wih support for this idea. It begins with a promise that those who understand it will not taste death. Those without this understanding are called 'dead' despite being biologically alive, which resonates with "let the dead bury the dead" in Luke 9:60. At the end, the disciples complain that Mary is not fit to receive Life because she is a woman (Christ disagrees). This indicates that receiving Life is something special.

All of this may seem incongruous in relation to Hadit, but just wait! All will become shockingly clear. For now, just be aware of this special form of Life. It is the major theme of this chapter.

If the capitalized word "Knowledge" in the previous verse was a reference to Gnosis, the uncapitalized "knowledge" here simply means recognition. When we identify with Hadit (Self-realization as the Khabs - Gnosis), we experience (know or recognize) the death of our persona or character as our idea of who we are. We pass through 'death' to Life (Zoe) - resurrection in the flesh.

Concerning the "flame" in the verse, it is worth noting the 'accident' concerning the Oil of Abramelin. Where the original recipe calls for calamus as an ingredient, Samuel Mathers mistranslated and substituted galangal. Crowley then further altered the recipe in the method of production, using essential oils. This results in an incredibly concentrated, fiery version of the Oil that can even burn the skin if not used carefully. In ritual, anointing oneself with this Oil can represent Self-realization with the Khabs and the presence of its Life and Holy Fire. This perfectly aligns with ancient Gnostic chrismation rituals that were a Baptism of Fire that complemented (and completed) the earlier watery one.

This is the Holy and Apocalyptic Fire mentioned throughout this whole Book.

7. I am the Magician and the Exorcist. I am the axle of the wheel, and the cube in the circle. «Come unto me» is a foolish word: for it is I that go.

The Magician and the Exorcist could further relate to the "the work of the wand and the work of the sword" in I:37 and to the Aeonic roles of Set and Horus as described in *The Book of Coming Forth by Night*: Horus, the Exorcist, as agent of the Purification making space for True Creation to manifest through Set, the Magician.

To Crowley's own comments concerning the axle, I would only add consideration of the Pole Star as the axis of the night sky (Nuit) and its reflection on Earth in the legend of the *Rex Mundi* or King of the World as personification of the globe's axis.

8. Who worshipped Heru-pa-kraath have worshipped me; ill, for I am the worshipper.

Nuit is the ultimate Object as Hadit is the ultimate Subject. Worship Nuit but BE Hadit. Worship Nuit AS Hadit, in His way. But also know this to be as your-Self, the Self specified in the next verse.

9. Remember all ye that existence is pure joy; that all the sorrows are but as shadows; they pass & are done; but there is that which remains.

The disidentified and untouched essential Self remains.

10. O prophet! thou hast ill will to learn this writing.

11. I see thee hate the hand & the pen; but I am stronger.

12. Because of me in Thee which thou knewest not.

13. for why? Because thou wast the knower, and me.

14. Now let there be a veiling of this shrine: now let the light devour men and eat them up with blindness!

15. For I am perfect, being Not; and my number is nine by the fools; but with the just I am eight, and one in eight: Which is vital, for I am none indeed. The Empress and the King are not of me; for there is a further secret.

16. I am The Empress & the Hierophant. Thus eleven, as my bride is eleven.

17. Hear me, ye people of sighing!

   The sorrows of pain and regret

Are left to the dead and the dying,

   The folk that not know me as yet.

18. These are dead, these fellows; they feel not. We are not for the poor and sad: the lords of the earth are our kinsfolk.

Reaffirms once more the elitist nature of the Path while echoing those Gnostic references to the non-Initiates as the 'dead'. This verse from Hadit matches I:31 from Nuit.

19. Is a God to live in a dog? No! but the highest are of us. They shall rejoice, our chosen: who sorroweth is not of us.

20. Beauty and strength, leaping laughter and delicious languor, force and fire, are of us.

The shift from death to Life is in Self-realization as the Khabs rather than being mired in worldly identifications - "the highest are of us" - and the Lifeforce of Hadit flows through. This is Zoe.

21. We have nothing with the outcast and the unfit: let them die in their misery. For they feel not. Compassion is the vice of kings: stamp down the wretched & the weak: this is the law of the strong: this is our law and the joy of the world. Think not, o

king, upon that lie: That Thou Must Die: verily thou shalt not die, but live. Now let it be understood: If the body of the King dissolve, he shall remain in pure ecstasy for ever. Nuit! Hadit! Ra-Hoor-Khuit! The Sun, Strength & Sight, Light; these are for the servants of the Star & the Snake.

Hadit's words in this chapter prefigured the Age of Satan. He refers to Himself as a Snake throughout and even borrows phrases from the Serpent of Eden. He speaks like Ragnar Redbeard, or Friedrich Nietzsche. Consider these words from Nietzsche's work *The Antichrist*:

"What is good? -- Whatever augments the feeling of power, the will to power, power itself, in man...What is evil? -- Whatever springs from weakness...What is happiness? -- The feeling that power increases -- that resistance is being overcome...Not contentment, but more power; not peace at any price, but war; not virtue, but efficiency (virtue in the Renaissance sense, virtù, virtue free of the taint of morality)...The weak and the botched shall perish: first principle of our charity. And one should help them to it...What is more harmful than any vice? -- Practical sympathy for the botched and the weak -- Christianity..."

And as Crowley exclaims numerous times in his own commentary: "The Christians to the lions!"

Indeed, Crowley comments upon this verse at length and quite well. It is only worth adding that the bodily dissolution mentioned is the disidentification with the Khu, and the solar correspondences provide ritual keys for invoking the extended spirit of Hadit into the Khu more fully.

22. I am the Snake that giveth Knowledge & Delight and bright glory, and stir the hearts of men with drunkenness. To worship me take wine and strange drugs whereof I will tell my prophet, & be drunk thereof! They shall not harm ye at all. It is a lie, this folly against self. The exposure of innocence is a lie. Be strong, o man! lust, enjoy all things of sense and rapture: fear not that any God shall deny thee for this.

Hadit identifies as a Snake several times and the chapter contains other touches of the Edenic Serpent here and there. In this verse, the wine and "strange drugs" are cast somewhat like the Forbidden Fruit of Knowledge, especially when paired with the promise that the partaker "shalt not die, but live" given in the previous verse.

But also, remember that in the Gnostic sense, the Serpent is also the Messiah! Like the Serpent - AS the Serpent - Hadit offers both the Fruit of Knowledge (Gnosis) and the Fruit of Life (Zoe). When we Self-realize as the Khabs (Gnosis), the Life (Zoe) flows down through the Khu in the Anointing that gives both words, "Messiah" and "Christ" - and this is the great 'heresy' and ultimate secret of Gnosis, that the historical Jesus of the vulgar churches is the counterfeit messiah and the Serpent is the true Christ.

Intoxication with wine and "strange drugs" has an established place in both tantric practice and the ancient lore of Set. After Crowley, though, the situation on the modern Left-Hand Path has been quite different with regard to such practices. Though he certainly appreciated alcohol, Anton LaVey understandably despised everything to do with the 'hippie' culture and was quite sour on the drugs popular with it. Following in his footsteps, Michael Aquino seems to have simply misunderstood the effects of these substances and the experiences that they can facilitate. Furthermore, neither would have wanted their organizations reinforcing lurid stereotypes or drawing unwanted police attention. And, of course, looming over the scene were greatly exaggerated depictions of Crowley's own final days as a heroin addict.

However, this is a new century and the scientific, therapeutic and legal landscapes for these "strange drugs" are now very different. A serious Left-Hand Path approach to the kind of work done by men like John Lilly, Timothy Leary and Terence McKenna is long overdue. There are two reasons for this. First, as said above, it is our direct heritage. Second, as various drugs like LSD, MDMA, psilocybin and cannabis become increasingly respected, legal and re-introduced to society, we want to be able to counter Right-Hand Path memes and philosophies that have become associated with them, lest they truly be misused to diminish consciousness rather than stoke and fan its flames.

Timothy Leary explicitly stated that he was carrying on Crowley's work. This is true not only with regard to this particular subject but also to his later, broader work in other forms of intelligence increase, personal and social evolution, lifespan extension and even space migration (unto Nuit, indeed!). Terence McKenna made looser comparisons between his work and that of John Dee.

These "strange drugs" are both revelatory of the

contents of consciousness and - to use John Lilly's language - useful in metaprogramming the human biocomputer. With regard to the metaprogramming, they could be profitably used in psychologically integrating the ideas and attitudes suggested throughout this Book and especially in this chapter.

Again, see Crowley's *Liber DLV* for an initial place to start with this.

23. I am alone: there is no God where I am.

An essential and ultimate Left-Hand Path statement, once more revealing the true nature of Thelema's proper expression.

24. Behold! these be grave mysteries; for there are also of my friends who be hermits. Now think not to find them in the forest or on the mountain; but in beds of purple, caressed by magnificent beasts of women with large limbs, and fire and light in their eyes, and masses of flaming hair about them; there shall ye find them. Ye shall see them at rule, at victorious armies, at all the joy; and there shall be in them a joy a million times greater than this. Beware lest any force another, King against King! Love one another with burning hearts; on the low men trample in the fierce lust of your pride, in the day of your wrath.

These are "hermits" in the sense of the alone-ness proclaimed in the previous verse. The rest speaks further against the asceticism of the Right-Hand Path variety. Remember also that Hermit is the first grade as given in I:40.

The Kings, then, are the successful "men of Earth" (the

third grade given in I:40), the "few & secret" servants of Nuit (I:10), which is emphasized by a repetition of the luxury, beauty and pleasure themes from Her chapter. These are the remanifested Daemons who have fulfilled the formula of Pandemonium as "key of the rituals" (I:20), and are thus literally Kings by definition.

In *The Black Ship* and elsewhere, I have talked about the importance of the Non-Aggression Principle as the true 'social contract' for a Left-Hand Path culture and civilization and the key to its realization. However, outside the non-initiation of force, do not be held back. It is a fact of life that there are many people doomed to fail, people who can not or will not be helped, and we should have no reservation or compunction about pursuing our own pleasure and fulfillment in life in spite of them. Thelema is not egalitarian.

25. Ye are against the people, O my chosen!

Quite.

26. I am the secret Serpent coiled about to spring: in my coiling there is joy. If I lift up my head, I and my Nuit are one. If I droop down mine head, and shoot forth venom, then is rapture of the earth, and I and the earth are one.

Highlights the distinction between Illustrative and Operative Magic, while also showing that they are complementary. The verse further seems to provide a definitive answer to the question of the Dove and the Serpent (I:57).

27. There is great danger in me; for who doth not understand these runes shall make a great miss. He

shall fall down into the pit called Because, and there he shall perish with the dogs of Reason.

This is not an instruction to reject Reason entirely - please, let us be reasonable! What seems to be at issue is more what Laozi called 'cleverness' (Chapter 65 of the *Daodejing*), meaning the mentally baroque, convoluted or sophistic.

28. Now a curse upon Because and his kin!

29. May Because be accursèd for ever!

30. If Will stops and cries Why, invoking Because, then Will stops & does nought.

The Mind is a machine with the purpose of securing and maintaining survival. Looking over human evolution and history, we can see where it has been both an amazing success and a dismal failure. Where the machine fails is in confusing the survival of the organism with the survival of the Mind, itself. That is to say, survival of the Mind's contents: its beliefs and identifications.

Crowley says: "It is the voice of Man, and not of a God."

Refer back to the comment for I:44, it speaks directly to this issue.

Also, we know Why: Indulgence (I:39).

31. If Power asks why, then is Power weakness.

This is the other side to I:44. Self-consciousness or indecision guarantee failure.

32. Also reason is a lie; for there is a factor infinite & unknown; & all their words are skew-wise.

The subconscious Will. Again, I:44.

33. Enough of Because! Be he damned for a dog!

34. But ye, o my people, rise up & awake!

Shift from the merely human perspective to the causative and divine perspective of Hadit.

35. Let the rituals be rightly performed with joy & beauty!

For Anton LaVey, emotion and aesthetics were the primary keys to Magic and this verse backs him up. Eschew rote ceremony.

36. There are rituals of the elements and feasts of the times.

37. A feast for the first night of the Prophet and his Bride!

38. A feast for the three days of the writing of the Book of the Law.

39. A feast for Tahuti and the child of the Prophet—secret, O Prophet!

40. A feast for the Supreme Ritual, and a feast for the Equinox of the Gods.

41. A feast for fire and a feast for water; a feast for life and a greater feast for death!

42. A feast every day in your hearts in the joy of my

rapture!

43. A feast every night unto Nu, and the pleasure of uttermost delight!

These last two verses emphasize the natural Magic in living, day and night (Sun and Moon). Otherwise, holidays of all kinds remind us to do so and can guide our attention in appreciating different aspects of existence. Every holiday brings us back to what Life should always be.

44. Aye! feast! rejoice! there is no dread hereafter. There is the dissolution, and eternal ecstasy in the kisses of Nu.

45. There is death for the dogs.

Another "No!" to the question in verse 19, and another reminder of Gnostic contempt for the 'dead'. Crowley's contemporary George Gurdjieff also warned against dying like a dog, and his work is well worth looking into for the serious Initiate.

46. Dost thou fail? Art thou sorry? Is fear in thine heart?

47. Where I am these are not.

These two verses re-state the nature of being Hadit. Fear, sorrow and failure are "shadows" as per verse 9 above.

48. Pity not the fallen! I never knew them. I am not for them. I console not: I hate the consoled & the consoler.

To pity the fallen is to identify with them and to fall along with them. It is that same fall from the throne or perspective of Hadit down into the realm of "shadows" from verse 9 and the previous verses, only now getting caught up in someone else's plummet rather than our own.

To Crowley's "Love under Will" (I:57), the members of the Fraternitas Saturni added the idea of Compassionless Love or love without pity for this very reason. Our Love for our Daemonic brethren should be expressed in sharing strength and not in mourning defeats.

49. I am unique & conqueror. I am not of the slaves that perish. Be they damned & dead! Amen. (This is of the 4: there is a fifth who is invisible, & therein am I as a babe in an egg.)

The Babe in the Egg is Hadit as Hoor-paar-kraat. He provides Life and Meaning to the Palace of Four Gates (I:51) and the world of the four elements.

50. Blue am I and gold in the light of my bride: but the red gleam is in my eyes; & my spangles are purple & green.

In I:60, Nuit decribed Herself as black to the blind but blue and gold to those with eyes to see. There, it was said that the blue and gold are representative of the wonders contained within the Darkness. They are the colors of potential daylight, the world of the Manifested. It is not surprising then to see these colors reflected upon Hadit, who we know is the manifester of Nuit. See again the comment to I:9.

There are many systems for using the symbolism of

color. In my own, and in the Mandala of my Dominion, purple and green are the colors of Elemental Earth and Water. These are the denser manifesting forces, and "spangles" is not a bad word for manifested phenomena.

While the association of the color black with the modern Left-Hand Path is more well-known, red is also very important. First and foremost, red is the color associated with Set in ancient times and Satan in modern times. Moreover, in the *Diabolicon*, we find an end and a new beginning in the Red Magus, that personage "who shall remake the Cosmos in the eternal glory of his Satanic Will" once "the Black Flame becomes Red in the glory of its perfection".

The red gleam in His eyes is clearly a sign of Hadit's essence and identity. He is the red circle placed within the pentacle or yantra also described in I:60.

Within my own system, red is still the color of Elemental Fire but has a special connection to the fire of the hearth, the heart and life-giving sun of the home. This may help to understand the Black Flame becoming Red, when it has been mastered in the same way that mundane fire was mastered and with commensurate results.

51. Purple beyond purple: it is the light higher than eyesight.

That I would make purple the color of Elemental Earth in my system is a key to the Magic of Pandemonium and has multiple factors supporting it. It began with a dream about my work related to me by a close companion. Once deciphered, it solved the immediate need to distinguish Elemental Earth from the broader concept of the Black Earth. Purple also makes Earth a more perfect complement to Air (yellow), as the change of Water to green did with Fire. But best of all, it marries the alchemical Violet Flame (most relevant to this verse) to the traditional purple of Royalty.

52. There is a veil: that veil is black. It is the veil of the modest woman; it is the veil of sorrow, & the pall of death: this is none of me. Tear down that lying spectre of the centuries: veil not your vices in virtuous words: these vices are my service; ye do well, & I will reward you here and hereafter.

Over a century later, I will just say that the connotations and relevance of this verse are very different and yet entirely the same. New cast, same old play.

53. Fear not, o prophet, when these words are said, thou shalt not be sorry. Thou art emphatically my chosen; and blessed are the eyes that thou shalt look upon with gladness. But I will hide thee in a mask of sorrow: they that see thee shall fear thou art fallen: but I lift thee up.

54. Nor shall they who cry aloud their folly that thou meanest nought avail; thou shall reveal it: thou availest: they are the slaves of because: They are not of me. The stops as thou wilt; the letters? change them not in style or value!

People will always find a reason to avoid or delay action and change. Any new proposal or idea is met with denial or doubt or questions of qualification. Go on, do the things. Success is proof (III:42).

55. Thou shalt obtain the order & value of the English Alphabet; thou shalt find new symbols to attribute them unto.

56. Begone! ye mockers; even though ye laugh in my honour ye shall laugh not long: then when ye are sad know that I have forsaken you.

As LaVey wrote in *The Satanic Bibe*: "Present yourselves to him who sustaineth the rottenness of the mind that moves the gibbering mouth that mocks the just and the strong! Rend that gaggling tongue and close his throat..."

This will become a fundamental point of the Third Chapter following.

Crowley equates this mockery with the unpardonable sin of the Christian Gospels: blasphemy against the Holy Spirit.

Those who mock or 'blaspheme' the Left-Hand Path and its Source ultimately mock and blaspheme their own Source, and they deny themselves the Life and other blessings of Hadit described and promised throughout this chapter in the process. They mock and blaspheme themselves.

57. He that is righteous shall be righteous still; he that is filthy shall be filthy still.

Revelation 22:11.

As human men and women looking for miracles in life, Hadit does nothing for us. But when we ARE Hadit, He gives everything and all things are done by Him for us and through us. We are then greater, blended or augmented beings. This is the major theme of the Third Chapter. But as we are told several times and know from our own experience: every man and every woman may be a star, but not all will take up this Inheritance and claim their Kingdom.

58. Yea! deem not of change: ye shall be as ye are, & not other. Therefore the kings of the earth shall be Kings for ever: the slaves shall serve. There is none that shall be cast down or lifted up: all is ever as it was. Yet there are masked ones my servants: it may be that yonder beggar is a King. A King may choose his garment as he will: there is no certain test: but a beggar cannot hide his poverty.

59. Beware therefore! Love all, lest perchance is a King concealed! Say you so? Fool! If he be a King, thou canst not hurt him.

60. Therefore strike hard & low, and to hell with them, master!

Crowley references Herbert Spencer in explicitly saying "The fittest will survive." No one can credibly dispute that Thelema is fundamentally rooted in what is commonly called Social Darwinism, even if the term (or its understanding) is flawed. Remember Compassionless Love.

61. There is a light before thine eyes, o prophet, a light undesired, most desirable.

62. I am uplifted in thine heart; and the kisses of the stars rain hard upon thy body.

In these two verses, it is admitted that the morality of Hadit is entirely contrary to the common and familiar morality of the Right-Hand Path, but it is also affirmed that those who integrate it will free themselves to Become as Hadit and will then experience the full flow of Nuit's affections.

63. Thou art exhaust in the voluptuous fullness of the inspiration; the expiration is sweeter than death, more rapid and laughterful than a caress of Hell's own worm.

64. Oh! thou art overcome: we are upon thee; our delight is all over thee: hail! hail: prophet of Nu! prophet of Had! prophet of Ra-Hoor-Khu! Now rejoice! now come in our splendour & rapture! Come in our passionate peace, & write sweet words for the Kings.

65. I am the Master: thou art the Holy Chosen One.

66. Write, & find ecstasy in writing! Work, & be our bed in working! Thrill with the joy of life & death! Ah! thy death shall be lovely: whoso seeth it shall be glad. Thy death shall be the seal of the promise of our agelong love. Come! lift up thine heart & rejoice! We are one; we are none.

67. Hold! Hold! Bear up in thy rapture; fall not in swoon of the excellent kisses!

68. Harder! Hold up thyself! Lift thine head! breathe not so deep—die!

69. Ah! Ah! What do I feel? Is the word exhausted?

70. There is help & hope in other spells. Wisdom says: be strong! Then canst thou bear more joy. Be not animal; refine thy rapture! If thou drink, drink

by the eight and ninety rules of art: if thou love, exceed by delicacy; and if thou do aught joyous, let there be subtlety therein!

Despite his criticisms and dismissals of most of Crowley's work, Anton LaVey taught this same approach to Indulgence. The practice of Indulgence not only runs through the entire Maslovian Hierarchy of Needs from the purely biological to the most intellectual and spiritual (Self-actualization), the fulfillment of each need or desire can be increasingly refined at each level.

As to "help & hope in other spells", remember the obeah and the wanga of I:37. The role of practical and results-oriented Operative Magic is in the tangible manifestation of desires, especially Deep Desires. This is the "rapture of the earth" in verse 26.

71. But exceed! exceed!

Pushing the envelope - which is not entirely a metaphor when considering the nature of the Khu.

72. Strive ever to more! and if thou art truly mine—and doubt it not, an if thou art ever joyous!—death is the crown of all.

73. Ah! Ah! Death! Death! thou shalt long for death. Death is forbidden, o man, unto thee.

74. The length of thy longing shall be the strength of its glory. He that lives long & desires death much is ever the King among the Kings.

75. Aye! listen to the numbers & the words:

76. 4 6 3 8 A B K 2 4 A L G M O R 3 Y X 24 89 R P S T O V A L. What meaneth this, o prophet? Thou knowest not; nor shalt thou know ever. There cometh one to follow thee: he shall expound it. But remember, o chosen one, to be me; to follow the love of Nu in the star-lit heaven; to look forth upon men, to tell them this glad word.

In ancient Phrygia, there was a famous puzzle: the Gordian Knot. Putting aside the story of how it came to be, the important points are that it was an elaborate series of tangled knots joining an ox-cart to a post, and there was a prophecy that whomever might undo the knot was destined to become ruler of all Asia. The day arrived when Alexander III of Macedon (known as Alexander the Great) came to inspect this famous knot and attempt a solution. According to legend, he drew his sword and sliced it in half with a single stroke. He went on to become ruler of all Asia.

77. O be thou proud and mighty among men!

78. Lift up thyself! for there is none like unto thee among men or among Gods! Lift up thyself, o my prophet, thy stature shall surpass the stars. They shall worship thy name, foursquare, mystic, wonderful, the number of the man; and the name of thy house 418.

See III:34 and its comment.

79. The end of the hiding of Hadit; and blessing & worship to the prophet of the lovely Star!

The Prince of Darkness - Hadit - comes forth autonomously from the womb of Nuit, revealing the Company of Heaven, those Stars who come forth in

His image. He gives us Knowledge and Life. This chapter reveals Him to us so that we can also be Him as instructed in I:6, so that we may fully manifest the wonders of Nuit. It gives us what we need to make full use of the devotional and magical practices sketched out in the First Chapter.

5

Liber AL vel Legis

Chapter III

RA-HOOR-KHUIT

1. Abrahadabra; the reward of Ra Hoor Khut.

Even with Pandemonium replacing Abrahadabra as the "key of the rituals", the latter formula still has meaning and value. Here, it is entirely appropriate because it is the magical extension of Hadit in Ra-hoor-khuit. Crowley comments that the spelling "Khut" rather than "Khuit" indicates a human conception, the divinization of which is indicated by the addition of the "i" to the Khu. That is to say, the divinization of a human being through a transformation of the Khu, enacted through the formula of Abrahadabra. This reward was described and promised throughout the Second Chapter and the process is explained quite clearly in verse 37 below.

For Crowley, that letter "i' is the Hebrew *Yod*, which is the solitary (isolate) Hermit of the Tarot. Further correspondences (from *Liber 777*) are Hoor-paar-kraat, the Lord of Yoga and the power of Initiation. The addition of the "i" also brings the name to 11 letters, as with Abrahadabra (and Pandemonium). Again, this is the essence and power of the monadic Hadit (or Khabs, as per I:8) to be magically extended throughout the Khu. ABRAHADABRA and PANDEMONIUM both describe the means of enacting this process and their connection to each other was made explicit in the comment to I:40.

To put it in terms of the mythology of the 'Osirian' Aeon, this "i" - this I - is like the sperm-seed of the legendary Watchers (or Sons of God) that engenders the race of Nephilim or Men of Renown ('giants') when mated to human flesh. We can now understand something like this legend much more clearly in light of verses I:2-3 and II:1-2 and their comments, which provide the key to making such things a living reality in the present day.

2. There is division hither homeward; there is a word not known. Spelling is defunct; all is not aught. Beware! Hold! Raise the spell of Ra-Hoor-Khuit!

Continuing directly, "homeward' indicates that Pandemonium is also applicable after all because it resolves the "division" as an integrated continuum. It conducts the force referenced above into the social and environmental dimensions in a necessary grounding and anchoring. The Black Earth remanifests the Black Flame. The even greater "reward" is in the fullness of the Kingdom.

However, see also the comment to verse 72 below.

Specifically, the "spell" is the divinization process described above as it is given in clear and lyrical form in verse 37. More generally, the proclamation of all that follows weaves around and through it.

3. Now let it be first understood that I am a god of War and of Vengeance. I shall deal hardly with them.

Hadit's lust for life and will-to-power collides with restricting cultural encrustations, producing an inevitable result.

Crowley knew nothing of war outside of poems, paintings and sagas. His disciple Major-General J.F.C. Fuller, on the other hand, literally wrote the book(s) on the subject and certainly with this chapter of this Book at least somewhat in mind. General George S. Patton was a devoted student of Fuller's work, which was something of a sad irony for the fascist Major-General. The nature of war definitely changed during this period, with Hitler preaching the doctrine of perpetual revolution, Goebbels speaking about the concept of Total War and the rapid technological explosion of new and deadlier weaponry (see verses 6 and 7 below).

While conventional warfare - or at least the use of its weaponry - is still very much a thing, I am going to say that the nature of war has changed again following the conceptual evolution that has happened through the Age of Satan and Aeon of Set, as well as simply a century of world change in general. This evolution in the character of our "god of War" is explained in the *Book of Coming Forth by Night* by the statement that the Aeon of Horus was a period of purification to create space for true creation under Set (see the comment to verse 35 for much more detail on this relationship). The new form of Total War that I advocate is prosecuted through BUILDING. Its destruction is creative, its disruption is transcendence.

THE GOSPEL OF PANDEMONIUM

I came to realize and embrace this conception of war in stages. My original interest, relevant to the previous chapters of this Book, was in determining how one might become and reign as an actual King in a world and age where the traditional means of becoming and reigning as a King have been made somewhat obsolete and rather difficult to put into practice. I was inspired by the (albeit Right-Hand Path) use of 'think tanks' and strategic philanthropy by Charles, Prince of Wales, and the Aga Khan. While I was experimenting with my own nonprofit organization, I learned about the book *Unrestricted Warfare* written by two Chinese military officers, Qiao Liang and Wang Xiangsui. This book expands from the use of 'think tanks' and propaganda to the use of international law, economics and the exploitation of networks. Later, Michael Aquino - a career military officer and the Magus of the Aeon of Set - released his book-length explanation of *MindWar*, which provides a useful structure.

From these elements, the new type of 'war' can be drawn out and put into practice on any scale, compounding gains to build up force and leverage, lessening the asymmetry between actants.

For example, consider the following from William S. Burroughs' novel *The Western Lands*:

"[O]ur policy is SPACE... anything that favors or enhances space programs, space exploration, simulation of space conditions, exploration of inner space, expanding awareness, we will support. Anything going in the other direction we will extirpate. The espionage world now has a new frontier."

Next, imagine - *hypothetically*, of course - that a

contemporary, decentralized 'hacktivist' network were to form around this mission statement and really take it to heart. Taking their plays from *MindWar* and using appropriate elements of *Unrestricted Warfare*, they might be able to do some very interesting things.

Ra-hoor-khuit's "War and Vengeance" are prefigured in I:52 and II:5. A recent operation is highlighted in verse 34 below. The new campaigns can be expected to play out on many scales and levels.

4. Choose ye an island!

5. Fortify it!

6. Dung it about with enginery of war!

7. I will give you a war-engine.

One popular interpretation of this verse in recent years is that it refers to the internet and world wide web. Not only do they have at least partial roots as a literal war-engine by way of ARPANET but we have also seen them play an enormous role in changing nearly every aspect of life, including politics.

Key technologies moving forward will be those that expand human consciousness and creativity and those that facilitate even more radical decentralization of power, especially in the areas of communication, law, finance and production (Johann Gevers' "Four Pillars").

As for myself, personally, I have received a most powerful weapon not unlike the storied Sudarshana Chakra, and I received it in a fashion absolutely in the character of this Book and its Magic.

Verses 4-6 relate to Pandemonium in the creation of an enclave that can be used as a place of leverage, but this should certainly not be limited to just one location or type.

8. With it ye shall smite the peoples; and none shall stand before you.

None of the technologies listed above are even commonly perceived as weapons.

9. Lurk! Withdraw! Upon them! this is the Law of the Battle of Conquest: thus shall my worship be about my secret house.

The "Law of the Battle of Conquest" is transformed as explained above by the nature of Pandemonium. Exoterically, the "secret house" refers to the enclave created according to the instructions given above. Esoterically, it refers to that House of Many Mansions that is Pandemonium in its essential form. See also the comment to verse 34 below.

10. Get the stélé of revealing itself; set it in thy secret temple—and that temple is already aright disposed—& it shall be your Kiblah for ever. It shall not fade, but miraculous colour shall come back to it day after day. Close it in locked glass for a proof to the world.

This would appear to be a straightforward reference to the actual, physical object, but Kenneth Grant ties the stele to things like Lovecraft's Shining Trapezohedron and Arthur Machen's Ixaxaar (or Sixtystone) as well as many other things. That might seem like one of Grant's flights of fancy but it also might be worth considering.

As a physical object, the stele would be a talisman at best, anchoring the synthesis of forces described in this Book as a whole. Indeed, Grant later calls it the talisman of the Aeon of Horus. What he does in his comment, though, is to consider the form behind the object. In doing so, he touches upon the greater, more archetypal thing represented by such manifold symbols as the Shining Trapezohedron and Ixaxaar stone, the Grail when depicted as a stone, the Perfect Ashlar of Freemasonry, the Chintamani stone, the Dragon's pearl and the Ace of Disks. The Stone of the Philosophers. This is the Black Stone, the Black Earth of Pandemonium in its perfect crystalline form. It is the Stone represented by *Samekh* - Jacob's pillow, the Coronation Stone - which Crowley chose to designate the crucial ritual in his *Liber DCCC*, which is discussed in more detail below.

Grant further uses his numerology to link the stele (stone) to the name "Zion", which possibly means "castle", but which Grant traces to an Egyptian word *senn* that he claims means "to found", "to establish", "to erect" or "to set up". The Black Stone is the Black Earth, the Kingdom or World-to-Come in the radical Left-Hand Path alternative to that proposed by the Abrahamic Zion.

Whether or not the literal instructions of this verse are ever carried out, these deeper considerations should be held in mind.

11. This shall be your only proof. I forbid argument. Conquer! That is enough. I will make easy to you the abstruction from the ill-ordered house in the Victorious City. Thou shalt thyself convey it with worship, o prophet, though thou likest it not. Thou

shalt have danger & trouble. Ra-Hoor-Khu is with thee. Worship me with fire & blood; worship me with swords & with spears. Let the woman be girt with a sword before me: let blood flow to my name. Trample down the Heathen; be upon them, o warrior, I will give you of their flesh to eat!

12. Sacrifice cattle, little and big: after a child.

13. But not now.

14. Ye shall see that hour, o blessèd Beast, and thou the Scarlet Concubine of his desire!

15. Ye shall be sad thereof.

16. Deem not too eagerly to catch the promises; fear not to undergo the curses. Ye, even ye, know not this meaning all.

17. Fear not at all; fear neither men nor Fates, nor gods, nor anything. Money fear not, nor laughter of the folk folly, nor any other power in heaven or upon the earth or under the earth. Nu is your refuge as Hadit your light; and I am the strength, force, vigour, of your arms.

The holistic view of existence and experience in the greater form of intercourse with Nuit - and the magical practices associated with this view - provide a refuge from the stresses of interacting with the effects of particular phenomena. The "light" of Hadit is the detached and unassailable perspective of Self as an essential monad described throughout the Second Chapter. These and the corresponding transformation of the Khu in Ra-hoor-khuit provide "strength, force, vigour" to our arms (capability).

18. Mercy let be off: damn them who pity! Kill and torture; spare not; be upon them!

For good measure, the voice of the Father momentarily returns through the mouth of the Son.

19. That stélé they shall call the Abomination of Desolation; count well its name, & it shall be to you as 718.

The Abomination of Desolation is mentioned by the Hebrew Prophet Daniel and later referenced by Jesus. It is usually considered to refer to an idol or act of idolatry especially and uniquely appalling to Abrahamic sensibilities, which would certainly apply to the stele as an object and even more so to what it represents. In this case, the reference might be considered somewhat humorous, but also quite serious. Another interpretation of the Abomination of Desolation is as a conquering army, which is quite appropriate to this chapter as a whole.

With this verse, everything that was said in the comment to verse 10 is also linked to this idea of the Abomination of Desolation.

20. Why? Because of the fall of Because, that he is not there again.

21. Set up my image in the East: thou shalt buy thee an image which I will show thee, especial, not unlike the one thou knowest. And it shall be suddenly easy for thee to do this.

This would seem to refer to an image of Horus. Crowley, himself, originated speculation concerning the god Set with regard to this verse, however; and

Kenneth Grant ran with the idea, assuming an image of Set and treating Set as the primary focus of the rest of this chapter.

I have had a different idea. It reconciles both, in a way, but goes in a new and bold direction. I now believe that this should be an image of the Red Magus, whom I first mentioned in the comment to I:21 and again with regard to II:50.

The Red Magus appears at the end of the Statement of Leviathan, which is at the end of the *Diabolicon*. Indeed, his appearance is at the end of the universe as we know it (see verse 72 below, which I take as further evidence), and is briefly and simply described as follows:

"Then the Red Magus shall behold only Leviathan, and he shall recognize that he has become the perfect mind, who shall remake the Cosmos in the eternal glory of his Satanic Will."

Red was the color of Set in ancient Egypt. Within the Temple of Set today, red is the color of the Adept. Within my own system, red is associated with the hearth. From these, I derive the idea that the change of the Black Flame to Red when fully mastered refers metaphorically to human technical mastery of fire, the day when our mastery of the Holy Fire of Ipseity and Sapience has become a technology equal to our mastery of mundane fire, electricity and so on.

The Red Flame provides the Red Magus with his title. We have seen this Flame emerge throughout this Book - beginning in I:60, through II:50 and culminating in verse 38 below. I now believe that there has been a comparable evolution and progressive revelation of this personage through the Aeon of Horus, Age of Satan and Aeon of Set. In the beginning, they are perceived as Ra-hoor-khuit or Heru-ra-ha (see verse 35 below). We know from the very first verses of this chapter that this represents a transformed human. In the Age of Satan, this transformed human is represented by the Red Magus. In the Aeon of Set, they might have been better understood through the Word *Xem*, had it manifested properly. Setians still contemplate the Red Magus within the Order of Leviathan, and a few still struggle with *Xem*.

The East is the place of RISING, where the Beast faces Babalon in the form of a Western Dragon in *Liber DCCC*. See verse 38 and its comment below, which are of great significance.

This has been one of the most profound revelations of this commentary. Its enactment in ritual has shown great promise and could potentially facilitate very dramatic Aeonic results over time. This ultimate Lord of the Left-Hand Path may also represent our own, personal Future Self.

22. The other images group around me to support me: let all be worshipped, for they shall cluster to exalt me. I am the visible object of worship; the others are secret; for the Beast & his Bride are they: and for the winners of the Ordeal x. What is this? Thou shalt know.

Within the Psyche, this describes the process of Daemonic Integration. In the outer, it is the power of the Mandala.

23. For perfume mix meal & honey & thick leavings of red wine: then oil of Abramelin and olive oil, and afterward soften & smooth down with rich fresh blood.

24. The best blood is of the moon, monthly: then the fresh blood of a child, or dropping from the host of heaven: then of enemies; then of the priest or of the worshippers: last of some beast, no matter what.

Beneath the symbolic language, the types of 'blood' in order are apparently: actual menstrual blood of the Scarlet Woman, the menstrual blood of the Scarlet Woman and semen of the Beast blended through intercourse, the semen of the Beast alone, either conjoined fluids or semen alone that have been charged with a specific magical purpose, the fluids of lesser practitioners, and finally - seemingly for rare and unusual occasions - fluids produced via homosexual activity or practices that are psychosexually antinomian for the participants.

25. This burn: of this make cakes & eat unto me. This hath also another use; let it be laid before me, and kept thick with perfumes of your orison: it shall become full of beetles as it were and creeping things sacred unto me.

26. These slay, naming your enemies; & they shall fall before you.

27. Also these shall breed lust & power of lust in you at the eating thereof.

The original Oil of Abramelin with calamus would have poisoned these (and made them far less flavorful), so the change had practical as well as

Aeonic benefits. Crowley notes that "lust" is probably meant in the older and wider sense of health. It is known that consumption of semen has health benefits for women, but one wonders if these benefits would remain with such small doses and after cooking. Despite Crowley's analysis of the actual nutrients in the cakes, the effect would likely be purely magical.

28. Also ye shall be strong in war.

29. Moreover, be they long kept, it is better; for they swell with my force. All before me.

30. My altar is of open brass work: burn thereon in silver or gold!

31. There cometh a rich man from the West who shall pour his gold upon thee.

32. From gold forge steel!

33. Be ready to fly or to smite!

34. But your holy place shall be untouched throughout the centuries: though with fire and sword it be burnt down & shattered, yet an invisible house there standeth, and shall stand until the fall of the Great Equinox; when Hrumachis shall arise and the double-wanded one assume my throne and place. Another prophet shall arise, and bring fresh fever from the skies; another woman shall awake the lust & worship of the Snake; another soul of God and beast shall mingle in the globèd priest; another sacrifice shall stain the tomb; another king shall reign; and blessing no longer be poured To the Hawk-headed mystical Lord!

On the Winter (South) Solstice of 2015 EV, at a sumble event that I had organized and that was graciously hosted by a friend, I explained to those in attendance that I had recently enacted a Curse against the stagnant legacy of Aleister Crowley, with the intent that some new life should spring from the wreckage.

Two days later, on the 23rd, Boleskine House in Scotland was gutted by fire.

Symbolically, the physical (outer) house would represent the mundane structures and trappings. At worst, this would include the superstitions and mere cultishness surrounding and barnacling Thelema - and the whitewashing. If so, the outer house had become an encumbrance obscuring the living, inner house. Though it was nowhere in my conscious thoughts at the time, I suppose that this commentary became inevitable the day the house burned - or the day that I spoke the Curse. We might consider the commentary to be the sword in complement to the fire.

Aquino, Webb and (to an extent) Grant have all commented at length on the relationship of the Aeon of Set to the Aeon of Horus. Crowley believed the "double-wanded one" to be Themis or Maat because of Golden Dawn ritual mechanics, but even he spoke of the hidden role of Set throughout the Aeon of Horus. We know, of course, that the two Egyptian scepters or "wands" called *Was* and *Djam* bear the form of Set.

The idea of an Aeon as an epoch of Time is a superstition, and the idea that they are regular 2000-year periods is even more of one. Aeons are qualitative, not quantitative. Though Crowley, himself, is to blame for the misunderstanding, he also had the wisdom to say: "[I]t may be a hundred or ten thousand years from now; for the Computation of Time is not here as There."

And concerning his confusion between Maat and the acknowledged role of Set, he also admitted: "It may be presumptuous to predict any details concerning the next Aeon after this."

We can go much further with this. The "invisible house" would be the house of the hidden god, Hoor-paar-kraat, who is identified with Set. It is the House of Set that stands with all obscurations burned away. I mentioned that Grant took everything that follows in this chapter as concerning Set at this point, and it is quite prescient when he says "The holy place of the Priest of Set is immune to all forms of attack..." as it was a Priest of Set who destroyed the outer, physical house and now further reveals the inner, spiritual one.

In his commentary to his own *Book of Coming Forth by Night*, Michael Aquino quotes a description of the Palace of the Prince of Darkness from the *Book of Enoch*:

"And I went in until I drew nigh to a wall which is built of crystals and surrounded by tongues of fire, and it began to affright me. And I went into the tongues of fire and drew nigh to a large house which was built of crystals. The walls of the house were like a tesselated floor of crystals, and its groundwork was of crystal. Its ceiling was like the path of the stars and the lightnings, and between them were fiery Cherubim amidst a background of water. A blazing fire surrounded the walls, and its portals were covered with fire.

And I entered into that house, and it was as hot as fire yet as cold as ice. There were no delights of life therein. Fear covered me, and trembling gat hold of me. And I quaked and trembled and fell down upon my face."

Michael Bertiaux, in his more basic works, describes a simple exercise of mentally travelling to the Holy House of the Spirits to enjoy their hospitality and learn from them. In practice, this is as simple as daydreaming. Indeed, it begins as daydreaming. We can use this description of the Palace to engage in the same practice, though without all of the fear and trembling. This is an excellent and easy means for empowering our minds and souls, but we must act upon what we learn to build our own outer house.

35. The half of the word of Heru-ra-ha, called Hoor-pa-kraat and Ra-Hoor-Khut.

In the *Book of Coming Forth by Night*, Set states that HarWer (Horus) is His own Opposite Self, created so that He might better and further define HimSelf. He explicitly says that He came forth in 1904 EV as that Opposite Self to create the Aeon of Horus as a period or force of Purification. He explains:

"HarWer I was when I was once part of the Cosmos and could achieve identity only by becoming what the Cosmic order was not. By HarWer I cancelled the imbalance, leaving a Void in which true creation could take form as Set."

If Hoor-paar-kraat is identified with Set, then Heru-ra-ha is equivalent to the god Antywey - Set and Horus conjoined in one. To Setians, this also corresponds to the Satan of the Age and Church of Satan as an overlapping of the Aeons of Horus and

Set.

However, notice that the verse uses the "Khut" spelling again rather than the "Khuit" one, as it was in the first verse of this chapter. Remember that this is the purely human conception of the Khu, emphasizing Horus as Man and Set (Hoor-paar-kraat) as the Divine when distinguished from each other. The conjoined Ra-hoor-khuit or Heru-ra-ha, then, is the understanding of the Red Magus that we have from verse 21 reaffirmed. And it was in that middle period, the Age of Satan, when the Red Magus was revealed to the world.

36. Then said the prophet unto the God:

37. I adore thee in the song —

I am the Lord of Thebes, and I

   The inspired forth-speaker of Mentu;

For me unveils the veilèd sky,

   The self-slain Ankh-af-na-khonsu

Whose words are truth. I invoke, I greet

   Thy presence, O Ra-Hoor-Khuit!

Unity uttermost showed!

   I adore the might of Thy breath,

Supreme and terrible God,

   Who makest the gods and death

To tremble before Thee:—

I, I adore thee!

Appear on the throne of Ra!

Open the ways of the Khu!

Lighten the ways of the Ka!

The ways of the Khabs run through

To stir me or still me!

Aum! let it fill me!

This is the "spell of Ra-hoor-khuit" that is to be raised as per verse 2.

"Unity uttermost" is the integration of the Psyche, foreshadowed in verse 22. The "supreme and terrible God" is invoked to "appear on the throne of Ra", which means to consciously become Hadit as instructed in 1:6. Daemonic Lifeforce (Zoe) - "the might of thy breath" and "the ways of the Khabs" - "run(s) through" to fill the entire being of the Initiate, transforming and divinizing them. It is a spell of Transfiguration.

To achieve this, we must work to "open the ways of the Khu" and "lighten the ways of the Ka" so as to facilitate that "unity uttermost" (integration). This is done by the resolution of complexes mentioned in the comment to I:44. These complexes are the "gods and death" that tremble before the "supreme and terrible God".

Recently, despite the clear and direct commands of I:36 and 54, certain misguided pretenders have altered the words "fill me" to "kill me". They offer flimsy, sophistic reasons, full of Because, that are easily dispelled by common sense. They ignore the fact that the text was published numerous times while Crowley was alive. Do they perhaps think that he would be unconcerned with mistakes? Do they forget that the formula of death was no longer valid? Moreover, it was Crowley, himself, who explicitly said the process was represented by the *insertion* of the "i" into "Khut". The prosecution rests.

Why would they do this? Because they are not Thelemites. Despite the clear Left-Hand Path nature of this Book, shown throughout this commentary, these people are Right-Hand Path in character down to the marrow of their bones. By changing a single letter - the very thing warned against - they subvert a moment of Left-Hand Path exaltation into a Right-Hand Path plea for annihilation. The "spell" is utterly blasphemed and destroyed.

Whether or not they ultimately receive the same treatment as Jesus, Mohammed and so on as given below, they will certainly be - and have already been - punished by simply *stopping*. They will not so much fail - because they would never try at anything - but merely never know success. Dead, as they wish. Moribund, torpid, stagnant and static. They are forsaken as the "mockers" of II:56. See also verse 57 below.

38. So that thy light is in me; & its red flame is as a sword in my hand to push thy order. There is a secret door that I shall make to establish thy way in all the

quarters, (these are the adorations, as thou hast written), as it is said:

The light is mine; its rays consume

   Me: I have made a secret door

Into the House of Ra and Tum,

   Of Khephra and of Ahathoor.

I am thy Theban, O Mentu,

   The prophet Ankh-af-na-khonsu!

By Bes-na-Maut my breast I beat;

   By wise Ta-Nech I weave my spell.

Show thy star-splendour, O Nuit!

   Bid me within thine House to dwell,

O wingèd snake of light, Hadit!

   Abide with me, Ra-Hoor-Khuit!

The Red Flame foreshadowed in I:50 and II:60 is now explicit. Refer back to the comment for verse 21.

Because of the reference to the four quarters or cardinal directions, Crowley believed that the "secret door" was the ritual in his *Liber DCCC*. This is the invocation of the Holy Guardian Angel or Daemon. It is designated *Samekh* which ties it to all the symbolism described in the comments to verses 10 and 19 above.

This is the place where the connection with Set is most

explicit, because the ritual was originally an invocation of Set in the form of the serpent (like Hadit) *Bata*, called "Holy Headless One" in the rite. He dwells behind the constellation Draco, which held the place in antiquity that Ursa Major (I:1) holds today. This ritual was re-written as the "Bornless" invocation in the Golden Dawn, and then Crowley further adapted it for his own purposes. The original version is known as the Stele of Jeu (hence *Samekh*, or stone) and is found in PGM V.96-172.

Remember that the Priesthood of Montu or Mentu was one that absorbed the Setian cult when it fell into disrepute.

39. All this and a book to say how thou didst come hither and a reproduction of this ink and paper for ever—for in it is the word secret & not only in the English—and thy comment upon this the Book of the Law shall be printed beautifully in red ink and black upon beautiful paper made by hand; and to each man and woman that thou meetest, were it but to dine or to drink at them, it is the Law to give. Then they shall chance to abide in this bliss or no; it is no odds. Do this quickly!

The Oath of the Magus is to make every action an expression of his Word or Formula. Crowley was not a Magus when the Book was written but it is as much as stated here that he would become one.

40. But the work of the comment? That is easy; and Hadit burning in thy heart shall make swift and secure thy pen.

41. Establish at thy Kaaba a clerk-house: all must be

done well and with business way.

Sound advice for anyone but especially for a poetic, 'trust-fund kid' occultist like Crowley. Magicians, generally, tend to be paradoxically poor with matters of business and finance.

But I think there is much more to this verse. Thelema seems to function best as a commercial venture. Its principles and many of its practices have spread most fully and effectively when disseminated through the Self-Help or personal growth industry. Direct engagement with Initiation and Magic will always appeal to only a minority, but most intelligent people can certainly apply the basic and practical ideas and techniques. This may be a further example of the "few & secret" ruling the "many & the known" as per I:10.

But I think there is still much more to this verse than even that. Economics in general is as rife with Right-Hand Path dogmas and superstitions as religion is. My belief is that education in the principles of economics - or, more properly said, catallactics - is of essential and crucial Aeonic importance. Ludwig von Mises said: "It is the philosophy of human life and action and concerns everybody and everything. It is the pith of civilization and of man's human existence." It is the stuff of invention, creation, value, desire and exchange. In this work, we are fortunate to have the tradition of Menger, Bohm-Bawerk, Mises, Hayek and Rothbard to serve us.

In his *Liber B vel Magi*, Crowley lists the Elemental tools of the Magus and gives the Coin for Earth. Quoting from my own comment on that text:

"The Coin is the Substance or Wealth of the Magician. With regard to the alternative symbol of the Pantacle, Crowley calls it the earthly food of the Magus in his Liber ABA or Book 4 (just as the Cup is the heavenly food). The use here of 'Coin' rather than 'Pantacle' or 'Disk' is noteworthy. A coin, as money, has connotations of value and exchange. Wherever a Word holds sway in the world, it establishes an economy of forces in alignment with itself. The same is true of any Initiate doing his True Will or Life Purpose, but the Magus entirely takes it to another level and scale."

In Milton's *Paradise Lost*, it is Satan, Mulciber (Hephaestus or Vulcan) and Mammon behind the construction of Pandemonium, and Mammon provides the substance. Milton also ascribes the paternity of Antichrist to Mammon.

42. The ordeals thou shalt oversee thyself, save only the blind ones. Refuse none, but thou shalt know & destroy the traitors. I am Ra-Hoor-Khuit; and I am powerful to protect my servant. Success is thy proof: argue not; convert not; talk not over much! Them that seek to entrap thee, to overthrow thee, them attack without pity or quarter; & destroy them utterly. Swift as a trodden serpent turn and strike! Be thou yet deadlier than he! Drag down their souls to awful torment: laugh at their fear: spit upon them!

"Success is thy proof" is also most excellent advice. Too often, something is accepted only because it sounds good but is never put to the test - or if it is, poor results or a lack of them are simply waved away because of intellectual attachment to the idea. When someone talks about ideas like these, look and see what they have DONE with them. Better yet, make your own test - this is how I ask you to judge this commentary. Turning it around, when you wish to share with others, let your results do most of the talking. The rest of the verse speaks for itself.

43. Let the Scarlet Woman beware! If pity and compassion and tenderness visit her heart; if she leave my work to toy with old sweetnesses; then shall my vengeance be known. I will slay me her child: I will alienate her heart: I will cast her out from men: as a shrinking and despised harlot shall she crawl through dusk wet streets, and die cold and an-hungered.

44. But let her raise herself in pride! Let her follow me in my way! Let her work the work of wickedness! Let her kill her heart! Let her be loud and adulterous! Let her be covered with jewels, and rich garments, and let her be shameless before all men!

45. Then will I lift her to pinnacles of power: then will I breed from her a child mightier than all the kings of the earth. I will fill her with joy: with my force shall she see & strike at the worship of Nu: she shall achieve Hadit.

Reading about the Scarlet Women in Crowley's life is quite sad. Certainly, he could be unbearable and horrific, but it is also true that women even today seem to often have a strange tether to conventionality that is less evident in men as a group. Far fewer women are drawn to Magic at all and they are an extreme rarity on the Left-Hand Path, especially.

This is unfortunate because it is truly the radical Individualism of the Left-Hand Path that so directly and perfectly addresses women's social issues as a group, while also best amplifying their natural and social power. It falls to the Sisters that we do have that they increase their rigor in our philosophy so as to communicate it to other women, as appropriate - but never for the sake of mere proselytization, and we must never water down our doctrines for the sake of popular appeal.

The punishments and rewards listed in these verses really apply to both men and women, the difference perhaps being in that women have both more to gain and thus correspondingly more to lose in reference to their historical status.

46. I am the warrior Lord of the Forties: the Eighties cower before me, & are abased. I will bring you to victory & joy: I will be at your arms in battle & ye shall delight to slay. Success is your proof; courage is your armour; go on, go on, in my strength; & ye shall turn not back for any!

47. This book shall be translated into all tongues: but always with the original in the writing of the Beast; for in the chance shape of the letters and their position to one another: in these are mysteries that no Beast shall divine. Let him not seek to try: but one cometh after him, whence I say not, who shall discover the Key of it all. Then this line drawn is a key: then this circle squared in its failure is a key also. And Abrahadabra. It shall be his child & that strangely. Let him not seek after this; for thereby alone can he fall from it.

48. Now this mystery of the letters is done, and I want to go on to the holier place.

49. I am in a secret fourfold word, the blasphemy against all gods of men.

Crowley believed this to be "Do What Thou Wilt", secret because different for every man and every woman, and the surest blasphemy against any and all gods. And it is important to remember that these "gods" need not be merely religious figures but can be ANY kind of Right-Hand Path belief system, institution or construct. That broader and more complete application is the work that still lies ahead of us, and is the fullness of the war and vengeance promised above.

This verse is a link between the Abomination of Desolation in verse 19 and verse 60 below.

50. Curse them! Curse them! Curse them!

51. With my Hawk's head I peck at the eyes of Jesus as he hangs upon the cross.

52. I flap my wings in the face of Mohammed & blind him.

53. With my claws I tear out the flesh of the Indian and the Buddhist, Mongol and Din.

"Din" is Ætsæg Din or Uatsdin, the Scythian religion. Simply a note, as I do not think anyone else was familiar with it.

54. Bahlasti! Ompehda! I spit on your crapulous creeds.

55. Let Mary inviolate be torn upon wheels: for her sake let all chaste women be utterly despised among

you!

56. Also for beauty's sake and love's!

57. Despise also all cowards; professional soldiers who dare not fight, but play; all fools despise!

The term "Armchair Magician" had not been coined yet.

58. But the keen and the proud, the royal and the lofty; ye are brothers!

59. As brothers fight ye!

60. There is no law beyond Do what thou wilt.

This is the 'prime directive' and Crowley says to apply it to all other laws and situations. Grant notes that the verse number, 60, corresponds to *Samekh* (verses 10, 19 and 38). The phrase functions as both a touchstone and alchemical Stone.

61. There is an end of the word of the God enthroned in Ra's seat, lightening the girders of the soul.

Hadit and the Ka as per verse 37: the coming into being of a Lord of the Left-Hand Path. where "end" is taken in the sense of *telos* and "word" is taken in the sense of *logos*. See the comment to verse 72 below.

This Lord of the Left-Hand Path is the Initiate who has Become as Hadit, mastered the Worship and Magic of Nuit, and now comes forth as a Man of Earth to wage war and take Dominion, thus Becoming a King. The ultimate type and end of this Kingship, I propose, is the Red Magus.

62. To Me do ye reverence! to me come ye through tribulation of ordeal, which is bliss.

63. The fool readeth this Book of the Law, and its comment; & he understandeth it not.

64. Let him come through the first ordeal, & it will be to him as silver.

65. Through the second, gold.

66. Through the third, stones of precious water.

67. Through the fourth, ultimate sparks of the intimate fire.

68. Yet to all it shall seem beautiful. Its enemies who say not so, are mere liars.

69. There is success.

Which is proof.

70. I am the Hawk-Headed Lord of Silence & of Strength; my nemyss shrouds the night-blue sky.

71. Hail! ye twin warriors about the pillars of the world! for your time is nigh at hand.

Set and Horus as described several times but especially in verse 35 above. Possibly also a riff on the Apocalyptic significance of Gog and Magog.

72. I am the Lord of the Double Wand of Power; the wand of the Force of Coph Nia—but my left hand is empty, for I have crushed an Universe; & nought remains.

THE GOSPEL OF PANDEMONIUM

The "Lord of the Double Wand of Power" would seem to be a reference to the same "double-wanded one" from verse 34 - but you will remember that was the one to come in the future, the one who would assume the throne. So this confirms an alternation in speakers, as Grant would have it, where verses 70-72 seem to refer to Horus, Antywey and Set in linear sequence. The wands are joined now, probably because they both have the form of Set. And indeed, the garbled "Coph Nia" is interpreted as *Xeper*, the Word of the Aeon of Set, by both Aquino and Webb in their commentaries.

The speaker may be Set, but might also be the Red Magus. Once more, I will turn to the Statement of Leviathan and ask you to consider the following:

"Only through obliteration of the Universe that is may man seal his mastery of the Black Flame, for only thus may he know that he is not subject to a greater Will."

In any case, the speaker of this verse says quite literally that this is the work of the Left-Hand Path - "my left hand" - and that it is there that new creation can take place.

73. Paste the sheets from right to left and from top to bottom: then behold!

74. There is a splendour in my name hidden and glorious, as the sun of midnight is ever the son.

The god Xepera - the Word *Xeper* - hidden (here) but glorious.

75. The ending of the words is the Word Abrahadabra.

THE GOSPEL OF PANDEMONIUM

Pandemonium replaces Abrahadabra not only as the "key to the rituals" but also here as the "ending of the words" - not in a final sense (although telic) but in a totalistic one. Pandemonium is not an Aeon but the matrix in which Aeons may come into being and exist. It supports all valid Words and Formulae and also absorbs and integrates them all within itself.

The Book of the Law is Written

and Concealed.

Aum. Ha.

Commentary by Edward Pandemonium, during the Thelemic Year of the Emperor in the docosade of the Hierophant, and my own "Year of Harvest", the first Working Year of Pandemonium.

6

Summa

The following is a brief summary of the much more in-depth Pandemonium Commentary to *Liber AL vel Legis*. It helps us to focus in on the essentials of what the text is actually saying and what it is advising us to DO, providing a guide and context for all of the information in the commentary.

I

The chapter concerning NUIT is Tantric and Magical. Our true nature and resurgence as Daemons is (apocalyptically) revealed and exhorted, while we are also put on the path of drawing our fundamental approach to existence and all of our Magic into a holistic relationship with the continuum of EVERYTHING perceived as a Lover. This relationship can be affirmed and celebrated by a ritual that is roughly sketched out over the course of the chapter, including descriptions of the roles of Priest and Priestess, various symbolic correspondences, a seal or yantra and even suggestions for incense.

Connected to this are all forms of sexual Magic and a program of exploratory sexuality aimed at the liberation and fulfillment of Deep Desire, as well as various mental (as in New Thought) and material (as in Hoodoo) practices that support the process. Beauty, pleasure and wealth are appreciated as both means and ends in Life and as sacraments of this Goddess, as well as rewards for Her worship.

II

The chapter concerning HADIT is Gnostic and Initiatory. The First Chapter instructed us to Become something greater through the model provided in this chapter, which gives us the secrets of True Being, Higher Life and Compassionless Love. Assimilation of these secrets within the Soul of the Initiate is complementary to the resolution of psychic complexes as described in the First Chapter. This makes us divine and deathless, and all the more powerful to manifest the wonders of Nuit.

We are also advised to push the envelope of our consciousness through the use of "strange drugs", which today brings to mind the work of men like John Lilly, Timothy Leary and Terence McKenna. A Left-Handed approach to this kind of work is not only called for but long overdue. The metaprogramming capacities of such substances can be a powerful aid in making the psychic shifts described in this chapter, and we must also stand to counter the deleterious effects of Right-Hand Path memes and tropes associated with these drugs as they are now entering the mainstream of society.

III

The chapter concerning HORUS in various forms is Yogic and Revolutionary - ALCHEMICAL - though I use all those terms very broadly. The hidden Initiation of Hadit becomes embodied. The Nightside Magic of Nuit becomes Dayside Action. The figure of the ultimate Lord of the Left-Hand Path stands as the model for the Kings referred to throughout the Book. The Flame of Hadit is to be fully mastered, the Wonders of Nuit are to be fully manifested and the world is thereby transformed - indeed, regenerated, as promised in the First Chapter.

After more than a century of great change in every area of life around the world, our new paradigm for War is through creative destruction. We are to dismantle and dispose of all Right-Hand Path belief systems and constructs, but we are to do so primarily through building and establishing their Left-Hand Path philosophical and institutional replacements. Economics and technology play fundamental roles in complementing our escalating battles for hearts and minds.

CONCLUSION

The moribund and stagnant legacy of the Book of the Law has been reclaimed, revived, rectified and remanifested in light of the further revelations of the Age of Satan and Aeon of Set, and in context with Pandemonium as the "key of the rituals" and "ending of the words" to inspire and inform our future action. Indeed the primary concern in doing this commentary was to draw out the keys to power and the instructions for using and manifesting that power. As a result, several new initiatives are suggested and we can also see how to better perfect those that were already in planning. Moreover, all of these activities and efforts may now be even more coherently integrated going forward.

The Black Earth remanifests the Black Flame.

THE GOSPEL OF PANDEMONIUM

7

The Princess

In commenting upon AL I:37, Aleister Crowley questioned the reference to the wand and the sword with the omission of the cup and disk. This essay looks at some answers to that omission in both John ("Jack") Parsons' relationship with the goddess Babalon and that of first Charles Stansfield Jones (Frater Achad) and later Margaret Ingalls (Soror Andahadna, or Nema) with the goddess Maat. I am not going into the histories of Parsons, Jones or Ingalls here, but am simply covering the main points.

What follows is rooted in a formula used by Crowley and his followers that is based on the name of the Hebrew deity: YHVH. As I wrote in my comment to AL II:5, I am all for scrapping Abrahamic concepts entirely, but this might be an exception in that the formula is really more about the Elements and the Tarot. What it describes is a family system of Father (King or Knight), Mother (Queen), Son (Prince) and Daughter (Princess). Babalon or Maat, then, is proposed as the Daughter or Princess that complements the Son and Prince, Horus.

Parsons' feeling was that the Book of the Law was incomplete because it did not fulfill the fourfold formula. It has no Daughter or Princess to complete and renew the cycle. He sought and received his *Book of Babalon* as a fourth chapter to complete Crowley's Book. Babalon was, of course, already a part of

Thelema. She is mentioned throughout Crowley's writing and has a place in a number of his written rituals. To fully understand what Crowley was trying to do with his cultus of the Scarlet Woman and Beast, moreover, one should also be aware of *The Two Babylons* by Alexander Hislop, which is recommended in the essay "De Natura Deorum" for the Ordo Templi Orientis. Today, Michael Kelly has done the most work in reinterpreting Babalon from a specifically Left-Hand Path perspective under the work of the Fifth Head of the Dragon in the curriculum put forward in his book *Apophis* and subsequent works.

Babalon stands out within the Thelemic pantheon in being rooted in legends of Semiramis and mentions in the work of John Dee while not being anchored to an Egyptian deity like all the others. While I think it is a mistake to try to interpret the Gods of Thelema in strict terms of Egyptian religious scholarship, we *can* anchor Babalon to an Egyptian deity and it does help to clarify some things. That deity is the goddess Qetesh.

Qetesh is an imported, Egyptianized, Semitic goddess that is usually depicted as a nude woman standing on a lion. She is representative of both sacred and sexual ecstasy. Qetesh is also associated with Astarte and Anat, other foreign goddesses given as wives to Set by the Egyptians. Esoterically, we can expand upon her role as a fertility goddess by understanding her as Fulfillment - the consummation of Desire manifest. Though the word *Thelema* is translated as Will, we know that it is Will as Deep Desire and not just basic willpower. Babalon as Qetesh is the cup to Set's wand.

The situation with Maat is somewhat different and

rather more complex. We have already covered Crowley's idea that the next Aeon to follow that of Horus would be that of Maat. Where Parsons initally looked to complete the formula with regard to the Book of the Law, the coming of Maat would fulfill it in the greater scheme of the Aeons, acting as Daughter to Isis and Osiris and sister to Horus.

The Aeonics gets rather tangled here, so we should remember that (as I wrote in my comment to AL III:34) the whole notion of Aeons as periods of time in the way that it is usually considered is a superstition anyway and we can simply disregard it.

Both Jones' and Ingalls' conceptions of the Aeon of Maat are mixed bags. Jones' Utterance was not the pure result of his own Initiation. Maat was pre-selected by Crowley and Jones took the grade of Magus far too early merely to satisfy questionable rules around Crowley calling himself an Ipsissimus. Where Crowley failed Thelema by failing to distinguish its Left-Hand Path nature, both Jones and Ingalls failed in being even more Right-Hand oriented than Crowley.

Nonetheless, both also saw important things. Jones recognized the key importance of the Mandala and also even expressed the fractal geometry of the World-Order in his "Macrocosmic Snowflake" diagram. His attempted Word, *Ma-Ion*, is concerned with Manifestation. This is the dominant theme in the message of Nuit, and the Word ties it to Maat as the Daughter of the Mother in the formula. Ingalls' *Liber Pennae Praenumbra* (Book of the Pre-Shadowing of the Feather) bombards the reader with various symbols but also communicates another Word to express the nature of Maat: *Ipsos*, "Themselves". This is from the same *ipse* - himself, herself, itself - that gives us the name for the grade or degree of Ipsissimus, but here made plural. She also made a connection between her "double current" system of Maat Magick and Chaos Magick.

So, with consideration to our limited space here, what is this all about and how is it relevant?

Maat was the Egyptian goddess of Justice, both in the legal sense that we commonly think of but also in a greater, holistic sense of Right Order. It is worth noting that the original title of *Liber AL* of the Law was *Liber L* of the Law, where L is *Lamed* in Hebrew and attributed to the Justice trump of the Tarot, which Crowley renamed Adjustment. The Law that it establishes in AL III:60 is Do What Thou Wilt, calling forth a powerful Adjustment in World-Order that is also great Justice in that it is an affirmation of Truth. The Word *Ipsos* - Themselves - takes the Individualism of the Law and extends it into the appropriate order for a company or society, both the Daemons of AL I:2-3 as the Hidden Masters or Secret Chiefs (Ipsissimi) and our mundane social order as manifested beings. The Word *Ma-Ion* - Manifestation - bridges those poles or aspects of who we are and further extends the Law into our relationships, institutions and culture.

The World-Order that is generated by a Law such as Thelema ordains is what is known in various sciences such as biology and economics as Spontaneous Order. This is the novel state or pattern that emerges from the free interaction of elements within a system. Spontaneous Order as a process allows for evolution through variation, competition, feedback and adaptation. It is dynamic and tends to overflow with abundance as many new and unexpected innovations emerge from its rich complexity. Examples of Spontaneous Order include ecosystems and free economic markets. To use the Word of the Magus Laozi, it is the Manifestation of *Dao*.

This is the earthly disk as Mandala, the pattern of wholeness, integrity and Right Order. It is a living Mandala, whose parts are ever-changing and so must also change as a whole through continual Adjustment. Maat is the disk to the sword of Horus, complementing and balancing.

So now, let us go back to the beginning and look at the formula again. In choosing to use the name of YHVH, both of the feminine elements are represented by the same sign and thus in some sense the same nature. Within Thelema itself, Babalon is the more concrete remanifestation of the abstract Nuit, which may be an esoteric sense of AL I:66 - "The Manifestation of Nuit is at an end." In the Aeonic scheme, Maat represents a more conscious remanifestation of Isis. The Daughter, be it Qetesh or Maat, replaces the Mother and inspires the Desire of the Father to initiate a new cycle.

As an aside, within the context of the Aeon of Set, this formula and these concepts are not used except perhaps on a personal level. For the Setian, Aeons are metaphysically understood more as layers of conceptual refinement, more akin to Dee's Aethyrs. In that sense, one might view the Aeonic progression of Isis, Osiris, Horus and Set as an evolution of conscious realization from the most natural to the most non-natural. However, even from this perspective, the relevance of this feminine remanifestation can be seen.

She replaces Isis as our foundation and inspires us to further creation.

So, yes, just as we find a composite Set-Horus in the third chapter of the Book of the Law, we can propose a composite Qetesh-Maat as its balance and complement. She is the Princess who becomes Queen and personifies the Kingdom. Moreover, this is not simply a pair of pairs but actually defines a sixfold web of Being and Becoming in dynamic Manifestation. This is the Mandala as Lamp and Pantacle conjoined in ouroboric loops of continual Becoming.

The Black Earth remanifests the Black Flame.

8

The Discovery and Recovery of Xaryomen

The need for a social and cultural reconciliation of stability and dynamism has been recognized within the Pandemonium Movement for some time. On the mundane level, this is reflected in our focus upon promoting decentralization, spontaneous order and antifragility. But on the more overtly magical side of existence, our strategy has been to access and harness the power of archetypal and archaic forces while also remanifesting them in forms appropriate to the present and future. Deep, ancient power sources for new (r)evolutionary machinery.

It was in keeping with this strategy that we began an investigation of Proto-Indo-European religion and found many resonant and relevant concepts waiting, but chief of these was the god *Xaryomen* (pronounced *cHaryomain*), the patron deity of these people and their culture. Xaryomen was not the dominant god of the pantheon in the way that *Dyeus Pter* (cf. Zeus/Jupiter), the Sky Father, was. Instead, Xaryomen was the god of their society, as well as of the things that held it together.

In the following summary, we will describe what Xaryomen represented, the extent of His overt and hidden influence even today and the relevance of this for the Pandemonium Movement, though that last factor is covered in more detail in the paper describingthe Xaryomen Mandala.

THE XARTUS

To begin, it is first necessary to be familiar with an idea that was of crucial importance to the Proto-Indo-Europeans: the *Xartus*. This is the World-Order, the structure of the Cosmos, often visualized as the roots and branches of a great Tree. The Xartus is a living and dynamic Order, not a static one, so the image of a living Tree is a good one. It is fed by the creative Waters of Chaos but provides form and substance to them. The seeds of the Tree's fruits fall back into those Waters and are later reintegrated into the Xartus anew.

Living and acting in harmony with the Xartus was supremely important to the Proto-Indo-European people, and its Cosmic Order was meant to be reflected in (and nurtured by) the mechanics of ritual, tribal laws and customs, and personal virtue and ethics. The Xartus could also be understood more deeply through the practice of divination.

Full understanding of the Xartus and its supporting principles is beyond the space available here. It is introduced, though, because its root *Xar* is shared by Xaryomen and that is very relevant. It more or less means "fitting together" and the Xartus is a pattern that fits together in a perfect way - "perfect" meaning both just and aesthetically pleasing. This is perfectly in accord with our own use of the term Cosmos, which really means "ornament" (why we also have "cosmetics"). We still see a surviving trace of this word "Xar-tus" today when we talk about "Kar-ma". In the case of Xaryomen, this root seems to have become the tribal or ethnic name of the people for themselves and was combined with the suffix *-men* that means something like "-hood" as in "fatherhood" or "motherhood".

So, what we have then in Xaryomen is a deified personification of the social and cultural principles and practices that facilitate living in harmony with the Xartus and by which these people chose to define themselves AS a People.

LINGUISTIC SURVIVALS AS CLUES

There are no Proto-Indo-European tablets, scrolls or other written media. To the extent that it is understood and talked about as a language today, it is as a result of reconstruction - of studying the evolution of languages and working backward. We can therefore now look at later mythologies and languages for clues to the nature of Xaryomen, and even find His hidden name in words that we still commonly use today.

If you had not guessed, the most direct survival and most well-known today is the politically sensitive term "Aryan" for what are now more commonly called Indo-Iranians (indeed, look to the very names of Iran and Iranians as a modern remanifestation of this name). For these ancient people, the name Arya meant "Nobles" or "Excellent Ones" and their texts provide the most immediate survivals of Xaryomen available to us.

The Hindu deity Aryaman was a patron of marriages, whose name means "companion", "close friend" or even "playmate". The Zoroastrian Airyaman is an even more intriguing figure. For one thing, as a common word, His name means "member of the group" which harkens back very closely to the original sense of Xaryomen. Airyaman is associated with both health and healing as well as following the *Asha* or Truth, a concept of central importance to Zoroastrian religion and related to the Xartus. Indeed, the Old Persian form is not Asha but *Arta*. These things will become more significant below, but we can already see how these early survivals can help us to understand deeper dimensions of both Xaryomen and the Xartus.

Later, and half a world away, we find the Germanic name Jormunr or Irmin as a title for perhaps Odin or Tyr and lending its name to the Irminsul pillar. The name is supposed to mean "great" or "strong" (or both) and we will touch upon this again below. Meanwhile, look also at the very term "German".

Moving on to simple words, the Greek *arete* is a term for excellence (originally defined as strength) that derives from our original root *Xar* and ultimately provides our contemporary words "aristocracy" and "aristocrat" - Nobles again (still). Greek also gives us *harmonia* - "harmony" - which not only again derives from the original roots but most nearly remanifests their original meaning. Perhaps most remarkably, we have the word "germane" that means relevant or fitting, but also kinship and even the relation of siblings. This word comes to us, though, from Latin for sprouts or buds (as in to germinate) and the meaning of kinship may refer metaphorically to buds of a common branch - as on a Tree!

So it may be that for a people to refer to themselves as the Xarya or some such may simply have meant "We are related and have ties to each other." However, there is clearly a double meaning due to the importance of the Xartus and the cultural principles and practices associated with living in harmony with it. Then, the more comprehensive and profound cultural statement in the name would seem to be "We are connected TO the Xartus and we are connected together WITHIN the Xartus - we are Xarya." From there, with the Xartus being Truth, living in harmony with it confers Nobility as well as strength and power. And so, we see all these themes popping up down through the ages as an increasingly obscured cultural stream.

ROLES AND RULERSHIP

Indo-European mythologies and societies have been divided by Georges Dumezil into three categories or functions: (1) Kings and Priests, (2) Warriors and (3) Farmers, Artisans and Tradesmen, and we can examine the role(s) of Xaryomen in keeping with this model.

The first function is further divided between Magic and Law. Corresponding to these, respectively, the first function deities best known to contemporary pagans are probably Odin and Tyr; and those familiar with Odin and Tyr might begin an approach to Xaryomen by contemplating a combination of their attributes. The earliest associations with the Aryan people and terminology are with Nobility and Priesthood, so Xaryomen may have been a primarily first function deity if this categorization scheme is accurate. However, being first function, being also a deity of culture in general and with wholeness and integration being implied by His very name, Xaryomen has connections to all three functions.

His connections to conventional warfare, though, are not overt. However, even though conventional warfare is still very much a thing, new forms of cultural warfare and 'lawfare' are emerging that are very much within the domain of Xaryomen's rulership.

With regard to the third function, Xaryomen is described as a god of Marriage and Healing, things that we see carried forward in Aryaman and Airyaman. These reflect the Xartus on the most basic levels of biology and the essential social unit of the family.

KING OF THE WORLD

We might even connect Xaryomen with the myth of the 'Rex Mundi' or King of the World, who according to legend rules from a hidden or subterranean throne. Esoterically, this 'Rex Mundi' is a personification of the 'Axis Mundi' - the Center of the World or Cosmos, connecting Heaven, Earth and Hell below, and around whom the phenomenal events of the World-Order turn.

More exoterically, the lands of those peoples reflecting a strong Indo-European descent or cultural influence in ancient times stretch from Iceland to Tibet. In modern times, this descent and influence has been carried to every part of the globe as a whole through first the formal British Empire and then the informal American one. In this sense, we can very truthfully call Xaryomen the King of the World through His people and their culture(s).

In fact, we can also easily connect the revival of Xaryomen to the myth or legend of the King under the Mountain. There are many local variations of this legend, but it always revolves around a King or Hero or Saint who has not truly died but only sleeps in a hidden tomb or cave and will return when most needed by the people. King Arthur, Charlemagne, Frederick Barbarossa and numerous others provide examples that can perhaps be seen as later and more relatable proxies for the forgotten Xaryomen - especially when it is remembered that the Mountain (like the Tree) is also one of the symbols for the world's center or axis and thus the Heart of the Xartus.

THE ALCHEMICAL ENGINE

Pandemonium is the Black Earth that remanifests the Black Flame. What we call the Black Flame is the Ipseity and Sapience of the Individual. The Black Earth is made up of the forces and substances of the world that have been touched and transformed by the Black Flame and which provide the context for greater Becoming. The weaving, transforming, alchemical engine that may produce the Black Earth is CULTURE.

The following quote describes a revelation of Xaryomen experienced by Ceisiwr Serith, the author of the book *Deep Ancestors* that has been our primary source on the recovery of Proto-Indo-European religion:

"I had a strong personal experience with Xáryomen in a

hotel in New York City. I was thinking of all the infrastructure it takes to support such a city — physical (roads, sewers, water pipes, electrical cables, telephone wires, etc.) abstract (laws, ordinances) and human (EMTs, police officers, fire fighters, road workers, bus drivers, etc.) I kept including more and more, and then suddenly, boom, Xáryomen was there, as the being incorporating all of that infrastructure, and not only that, but the society that the infrastructure supports."

Pandemonium defines a continuum of Psychic, Social and Material Dimensions. It integrates the Individual, the society of Individuals and their environments together into the context of living and Becoming. We can see from all of the above and from this contemporary vision of Xaryomen's continued (if obscured) presence, that of all mythic figures or ideals, He seems to be most resonant with what Pandemonium expresses. He began as an archaic and tribal god, but is yet more inclusive than any other comparable figure could be when applied to the population of the world today - and it is in His nature to be more inclusive yet. He comes from the distant past but can easily be remanifested in a form that is relevant to the present and the distant Future.

In daily life, Xaryomen is a god of Marriage and Healing. In the metaphysical domain, this is because Xaryomen is a god of Integration and Regeneration. He is the god of the Xartus and its Power. Likewise, Xaryomen may be seen as a manifestation of the Spirit of the Mandala and a great force for Pandemonium.

9

Introduction to the Xaryomen Mandala

The Xaryomen Mandala was developed to serve as the ritual foundation of the Mass of Xaryomen. The word "developed" is used because it was a mixed process of creation, discovery and inspiration. Independent of the Mass, the Xaryomen Mandala is a particular manifestation of the Mandala archetype and also functions as an operative sigil or seal.

The Mandala contains several types of objects and substances but is mostly made from candles. These candles represent archaic Proto-Indo-European deities and give them substance (wax) and presence (fire) as well as also being offerings of substance and energy to them. Pillar candles are recommended, with the central candle being slightly taller than the others. For home use or small gatherings, 3x3 and 3x6 inches are very good sizes. These pillar candles make the Mandala look and feel substantial as well as reinforcing an idea of the Pillars of the Kingdom.

The arrangement of candles within the Xaryomen Mandala is as follows:

NORTH: This is the quadrant of Yemos, the King of the Dead. The Hindu Yama and Norse Ymir both derive from Yemos. Under Yemos, this Pillar is also for all the Ancestors and Honored Dead. Especially honored in the Mass of Xaryomen are the *Wikpotes*, the very ancient Kings or Chieftains. The candle is purple and also represents the Moon and Elemental Earth.

WEST: The quadrant of Xakwom Nepot, Lord of the Waters, remembered later as the Vedic/Avestan Apam Napat and the Roman Neptune. In His most ancient form, He is the Guardian of the Well of Chaos, so we associate Him here with the *Hogwhes* - the Outsiders. Commonly labeled as 'snakes' these are beings outside of the World-Order as humans understand it. This candle is green and also represents Venus and Elemental Water.

SOUTH: This is the quadrant of Paxuson, later a solar deity called Pushan in India, and whose original qualities split into Hermes and Pan under the Greeks - both protector of herds and patron of commerce (as well as psychopomp). The spirits under Paxuson are like satyrs and nymphs (or incubi and succubi) crossed with the imagery of angels - something like the Etruscan *Lasae*. Messengers and connectors, guardians of roads and their crossings. The candle is yellow and also represents the Sun and Elemental Air.

EAST: The quadrant of Westya, from whom most obviously derive Greek Hestia and Roman Vesta. As the Sun (which rises in the East) warms and gives life to the world as a whole, so the hearth-fire of Westya does to the home. Under Her are all manner of helpful and industrious household and homestead spirits. The candle is red and also represents Mars and Elemental Fire.

CENTER: The Center is Xaryomen as both the Source

and synthesis of all the others. The candle is black and further represents both the Black Flame and the Black Earth, as well as the connection between them.

We face the Mandala from the West and toward the East, following the archaic tradition. To the left, between the stations of Xayomen and Yemos, we place a horse figurine facing East. To the right, between the stations of Xaryomen and Paxuson, we place a cow figurine facing West. The horse is for Hekwona (cf. Gaulish Epona) and the cow is for Gwouwinda (cf. Hindu Govinda). These deities represent a dichotomy of feminine energies, conferring Sovereignty and Sustenance respectively. Their placement represents a dynamic balance of these forces and their circulation within and throughout the World-Order expressed by the Mandala.

Forefront, between the stations of Xaryomen and Xakwom Nepot, there is a cup containing Nekter, the Sacred Drink. This word was also used by the Greeks for a food or drink of the Gods and survives today in English as "nectar", but the Sacred Drink has other descendents in the Vedic Soma, Avestan Haoma and the poetic mead of the Germanic peoples. The cup also represents the Well of Chaos and some kind of high-proof alcohol is recommended for most operations. Opposite this, between the stations of Xaryomen and Westya, is placed some ghee (preferably) or butter - the literal Fat of the Land. These substances are consumed in the Mass of Xaryomen after the horse and cow are anointed with some of the Nekter and ghee, respectively.

Taken as a whole, the Xaryomen Mandala combines an enormous amount of metaphysical, mythological and archetypal information and distills it into a relatively simple form. Opposites of Chaos and Cosmos, Masculine and Feminine, Planets, Elements and even color are placed into balance with Xaryomen as the Center - a paradoxically dynamic equilibrium representative of the living World-Order.

Shamanically, the Center is where all places and times are One. As in the physics of David Bohm, we might say that it is the Implicate Order, while the periphery is the Explicate Order. Xaryomen bridges the two and His place at the Center underlines His role as a deity of both Marriage and Healing, as well as being the personification of the Culture. In a state of tensegrity, Xaryomen empowers and sustains the other deities as they empower and sustain Him.

Ultimately, the Xaryomen Mandala is a pattern or field of metaphysical, mythological and archetypal energies given material substance in the mesocosm so that it may simultaneously remanifest in both the microcosm and macrocosm. It is an all-healing *panacea* and empowerment applied to every aspect of both the personal Psyche and the whole of the World-Order. As such, its creation and use in the Mass of Xaryomen is thus the most perfect and TOTAL operation of Magic.

10

THE MASS OF XARYOMEN

0. Establish the Mandala and be seated in the West. Proclaim the following.

1. I call forth the Deep Gods of my Blood and the Deep Magic of the Noble Folk to empower me, to regenerate the World and to manifest the Black Earth that remanifests the Black Flame: PANDEMONIUM!

2. [NORTH: Light candle.] Spirit of Earth, come forth! In your station, I also call forth and honor Yemos, the Great King of the Dead, who rules over the Spirits of the Dead; and under Yemos, I call forth and honor the Wikpotes - the Ancestral Kings and Chieftains, Lords of the Household - and all the Ancestors and Honored Dead. Create DOMINION for Xaryomen! Create DOMINION for me!

3. [WEST: Light candle.] Spirit of Water, come forth! In your station, I also call forth and honor the Kinsman of the Waters, Xakwom Nepot, the Guardian of the Well of Chaos at the Center of the World; and under Xakwom Nepot, I also call forth and honor the Hogwhes, the Outsiders, those wonderful Spirits of Magic who appear in draconian forms from beneath the Primal Waters. Give LIFE to Xaryomen! Give LIFE to me!

4. [SOUTH: Light candle.] Spirit of Air, come forth! In

your station, I also call forth and honor Paxuson - the keeper of herds and flocks, protector of travellers and guide of souls; Opener and Guardian of all Roads and Ways, Giver of Prosperity! And under Paxuson, I also call forth and honor those sylphan satyrs and nymphs, winged fates and aerial Xansus of Eros who can forge connections within and between worlds. OPEN the WAYS for Xaryomen! OPEN the WAYS for me!

5. [EAST: Light candle.] Spirit of Fire, come forth! In your station, I also call forth and honor Westya, the living fire of the hearth. As the sun gives life to the world, the hearth gives life to the Home. Under Westya, the heart and sun of the Home, I also call forth and honor all the helpful and productive Spirits of the Household. Create a HOME and FAMILY for Xaryomen! Create* a HOME and FAMILY for me! (*Or maintain/sustain.)

6. [CENTER: Light candle. Trace the Pentagram counter-clockwise from its downward tip as you pronounce the formula ZAZAS ZAZAS NASATANADA ZAZAS.] Spirit of the Black Flame, come forth! Spirit of the Black Earth, come forth! Here in the Center, I also call forth and honor Xaryomen, who is Nobility and Soul of the Noble Blood and Culture. Xaryomen, be the Axis and Bridge that joins the Black Flame and the Black Earth! Xaryomen, create the Axis and Bridge that joins the Black Flame and the Black Earth!

Return and Remanifest, Xaryomen! Return and Remanifest within me! Return and Remanifest throughout the World! Joining distant past and distant Future, return and Remanifest! Joining fertile lands and farthest stars, return and Remanifest! Sovereignty,

Sustenance, Strength, Substance!

7. Lords of the Left-Hand Path and all allies of Pandemonium throughout Time and Space, as well as all Spirits of Fortune and Providence: Come, Come, Come to my help and hear me! I ask the help and presence of the Spirits and I call upon all Beings of Magical Renewal and Transformation to aid and assist me. I honor all of the Spirits of Chaos and Cosmos together - and with your help, I work to spread the Black Earth of Pandemonium beneath our feet.

8. The Pillars of the Kingdom are established. The Fourfold Wheel of unfolding Well-Being is set in motion. Here and Now, all that I have called come together to support and enhance each other, and Xaryomen reigns. It is GOOD. [Pause to appreciate the Mandala.]

9. [Place hand upon the vessel of Nekter.] Medium of Holy Spirits of the Waters below and beneath all Worlds, of the Spirits of the Dead and the Seas and the Roads and the Household, I consecrate and serve to you this Holy Nekter in offering. Receive this service.

10. [Trace rim of glass three times counterclockwise.] The Well reaches down into the Depths. The Well rises up from the Depths. Fire that falls, Water that rises. From the One, the Other; from the Other, the One. From both combined, Fire in Water, the Hidden Mystery here revealed.

Source of Life to all who drink it, Source of Power to all who drink it, Source of Holiness to all who drink it - from the Well of Xakwom Nepot, the Gift of Nekter is offered. Drink and be filled with the

Water-that-Burns.

[Anoint horse figurine.] Hekwona, give Sovereignty.

11. Clarified butter is the purest gold of the cow, truly the fat of the land. I consecrate and serve to you this Earthly Gift of essential and powerful Nourishment in offering. Receive this service. Eat and be given Substance.

[Anoint cow figurine.] Gwouwinda, give Sustenance.

12. Let my Body be as one with the Xartus and the World-Tree. As I feed and regenerate my Body with Sacred Drink and Sacred Food, I feed and regenerate the World-Tree and the Xartus with Sacred Drink and Sacred Food - HEALING ALL.

I am like both Mannos and Yemos in One. Like Mannos, I am the Primordial Priest. Like Yemos, my Body becomes the Cosmos. My blood, the waters. My bones, the rocks. My flesh, the soil. My hair, the plants. My eyes, the sun and moon. My brain, the clouds. My skull, the sky. May everything go to its place. May all things be as they should. By this rite, I craft the World from my own Being.

13. I draw into my Being all the Powers of Chaos and Cosmos and join them together. [Drink. Eat.]

[The Work of Inner Vision]

The World-Tree has been fed and healed and renewed. The Xartus has been fed and healed and renewed. Here at the Center, Chaos and Cosmos are joined together, both renewed.

THE GOSPEL OF PANDEMONIUM

It is GOOD.

14. I have added flames unto Fire, and given my words to the Air. I have poured Nekter into the rivers of Blood and Water, and I have provided the Substance of wax and clarified butter to the Earth. My ritual is woven into the Xartus and Xaryomen reigns. It is well done. The Black Earth remanifests the Black Flame: PANDEMONIUM!

[Extinguish Flames in reverse of the order that they were lit.]

15. [Clap thrice.] So be it.

THE GOSPEL OF PANDEMONIUM

11

THE FOUNDATIONS OF NOBILITY

Because the Left-Hand Path is rooted in the personal cultivation of excellence and achievement, its mood and style are implicitly elitist and aristocratic. It says something of our age that these terms have fallen into disfavor but they are used here in their purest sense, connoting the greatest health and goodness. We often speak of Nobility on the Path, and the purpose of this essay is to define what that Nobility is and to distinguish it from Right-Hand Path degradations rooted in demiurgic authority and mere legal inheritance. It is a call to the Nobles that it describes so that they may both come into being and come together upon the Black Earth.

This is another operative lesson that we can draw from the Deep Ancestors. The descendants of the Proto-Indo-European people called themselves Arya, which means Noble in the sense of honor and excellence. The PIE people may have previously called themselves something similar. In the first essay of this series, the name Xarya was put out there for the sake of argument. English "noble" derives from the idea of being noted or distinguished, coming from the same root as "known". The present cult of celebrity could be seen as a degenerate substitute for Nobility in that sense. But the nobility of "Arya" or "Xarya" is something antecedent and causative to its renown   -

the truly Noble are not simply famous for being famous.

After looking in that essay at a variety of related names and words from a variety of places and times, we found basic recurring themes of excellence and strength. We said then that the inner meaning of this name could be considered to derive from connection to and within the Xartus, because living in alignment with it as Truth would result in glory, power and success for the people as a group. To further explain this now, we can add that this relationship was enacted concretely through structural principles or sub-elements of the Xartus called Swartus, Swedhos, Dhetis and Yewesa that will be described below and which can be applied to our work today.

First, let us briefly recall that the Xartus is the World-Order, the structure of the Cosmos, often visualized as the roots and branches of a great Tree. The Xartus is not static but a living and dynamic Order, so the image of a living Tree is a good one. It is fed by the creative Waters of Chaos and provides form and substance to their power, while the seeds of the Tree's fruits eventually fall back into those Waters and are again remanifested through the Xartus anew. Looking closely into our own existence within the Xartus, we can see that it has several dynamics that we can actively engage with in daily living. These were listed above and we can now look at them in more detail.

SWARTUS is the particular focus and reflection of the Xartus within a specific person. With the Xartus being often symbolized by a Tree, our personal Swartus would be our manifestation as a twig of that Tree.

From the Right-Hand Path, the Swartus would be viewed in terms of all the externally-derived things - genetics, culture, education, relationships, life experiences and so on - that shape our Being and our personalities as their synthesis. However, from the Left-Hand Path we are conscious of our agency and volition in the intentional re-shaping of these elements and our resultant Being. Remembering that the greater Xartus is a dynamic and living order that we may also work to consciously shape, we begin here with the Swartus and work our way outward. Our concepts of Deep Desire and True Will are essential parts of the Swartus.

SWEDHOS are ethics. These are the principles of action that maximize the benefits of our existence by harmonizing Swartus with Xartus and most especially in terms of our social relations and interactions. For the PIE people, the most important of these principles were Truth (clear knowledge of the Xartus), Justice (appropriate action with regard to Truth) and Hospitality (or exchange, conditioned by Truth and Justice). Today, we have the Non-Aggression Principle prohibiting the initiation of force as both a distillate of these principles and a clarifying and unifying guide for them.

DHETIS are the laws that maintain social order. For example, in contrast to our current statutory law, the gradual and proximate evolution of common law better reflects the nature of the Xartus and also tends to recognize and most respect the Swartus of each Individual within society. That is, as a process of creating law and not necessarily in reference to specific laws of the past. Under Left-Hand Path principles, the Dhetis would certainly not contradict the Swartus but would simply codify the most basic and clearly recognized of the corresponding Swedhos.

YEWESA are the principles of ritual activity that best align with the functioning of the Xartus for either influencing or divining it. For example, because Creation began with the sacrifice of Yemos, whose body was used to make the world and cosmos, sacrifice is an important part of PIE (and descendant) religious ritual. Also, because hospitality and exchange are important virtues, sacrifice is additionally seen as both hospitality to the Gods and exchange with them. Yewesa also apply to rituals that have the specific purpose of affirming the Xartus as a whole, of which our Mass of Xaryomen would be a new example (in which the given examples of sacrifice and exchange are now understood and enacted more esoterically, if no less substantially).

These are very ancient things but still immediately relevant to our existence today. Even religious ritual, which has declined tremendously in an overt sense, persists in new forms that reify and support the new objects of popular devotion. And so, just as in the most ancient of times, we create our Nobility today through our conscious and refined activity in each of these areas. Through that activity, we become Noble in both the sense of being honorable and the sense of outstanding fame or renown (reputation). We transform our Being and existence into an integrated and holistically uplifting force. We do this through the combination of Vision and Deeds.

Moreover, the doctrines of the Left-Hand Path in practice and of Pandemonium as its contextual *telos* give informed precision to these aims. Left-Hand Path

Initiation has defined itself by its developmental focus on what is here called the Swartus and the corresponding magical elements or Yewesa of its structure. Pandemonium has come to help clarify and explicate the Swedhos, Dhetis and further Yewesa of the social and environmental matrices that may best encourage and support that focus.

Further, we are most fortunate in this Work to have the technology of the Magical Oath to focus our Being and Will in these areas and to initiate right expressive action within them.

There are three Magical Oaths that facilitate access to and expression of Nobility within Pandemonium. The First Oath is the one made to one's own Daemon as given in *The Black Ship*. In the language of this essay it binds our loyalty to the Truth of our own Swartus, and it is the root of everything.

The Second Oath is to apply the Non-Aggression Principle (also described in *The Black Ship*) in all our dealings with others, as the guiding rule of our Swedhos and Dhetis. It respects the Swartus of each person and most appropriately harmonizes it with others within the Xartus.

The Third Oath is a pledge to act as a dedicated agent of Pandemonium in the greater world beyond our own private lives. This ultimate Oath commits one to all of the noble principles even more deeply. The First and Second Oaths are suitable for anyone and everyone. The Third Oath will only be appropriate for some, insofar as it resonates with their own Swartus.

The Xartus is a dynamic order, not a fixed one. Our

actions are woven into it and become a part of it. The kind of Nobility described here is a quality of our actions. To be Noble is something we Become through what we DO every day. These principles and Oaths show us how to do this. In the process, we transform the Xartus. It becomes Pandemonium.

The Black Earth remanifests the Black Flame.

www.ingramcontent.com/pod-product-compliance
Lightning Source LLC
Chambersburg PA
CBHW070430010526
44118CB00014B/1975